A Pre-Raphaelite Journey

The Art of Eleanor Fortescue-Brickdale

Pamela Gerrish Nunn

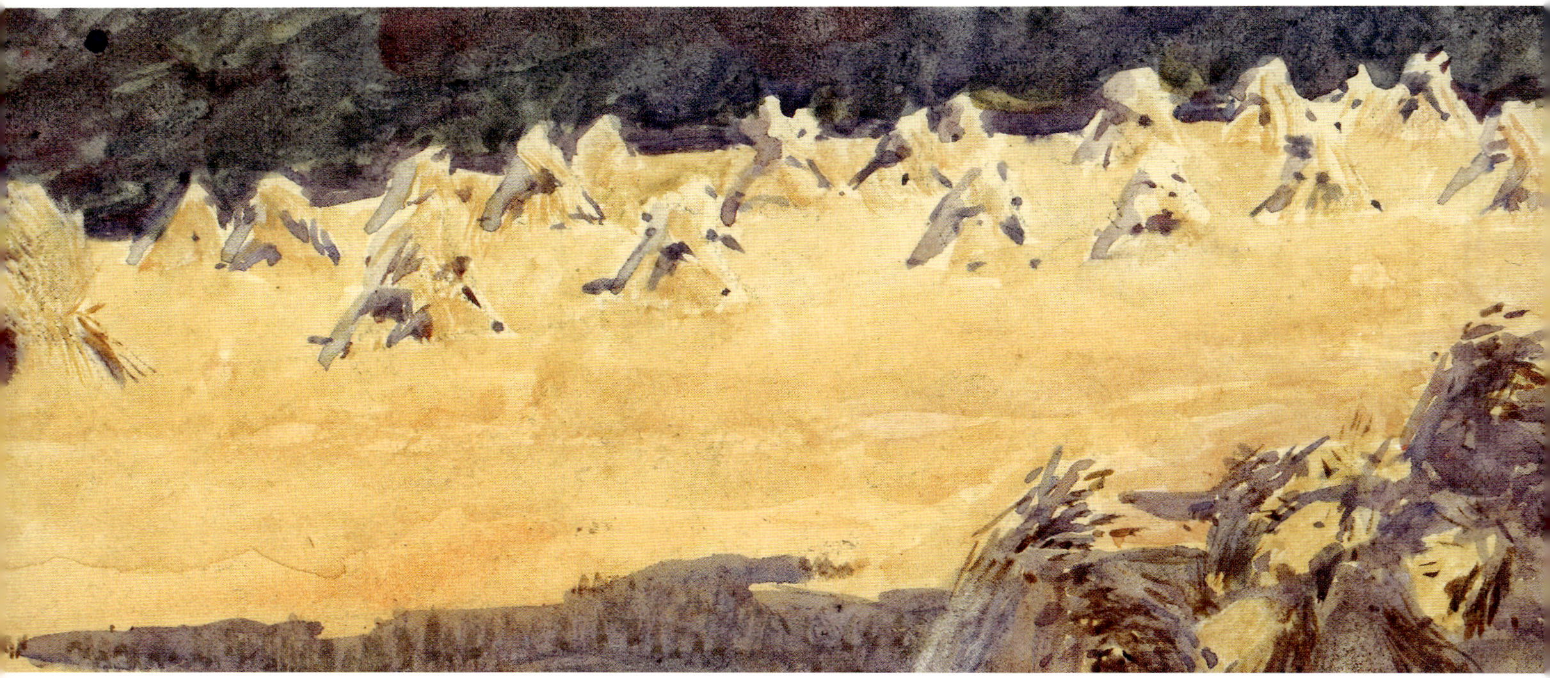

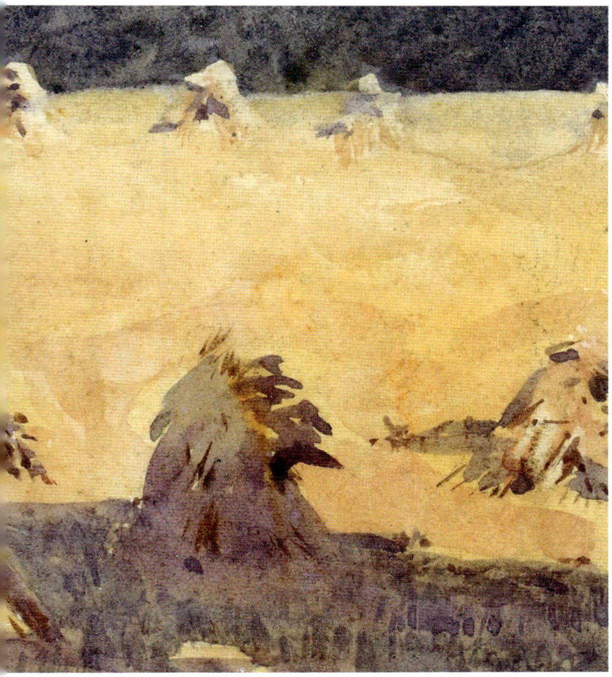

A Pre-Raphaelite Journey

The Art of Eleanor Fortescue-Brickdale

Pamela Gerrish Nunn

Published by
Liverpool University Press
4 Cambridge Street
Liverpool
L69 7ZU

and

National Museums Liverpool
127 Dale Street
Liverpool
L2 2JH

ISBN 978-1-84631-857-3

Printed and bound in the UK by
Henry Ling Ltd

Contents

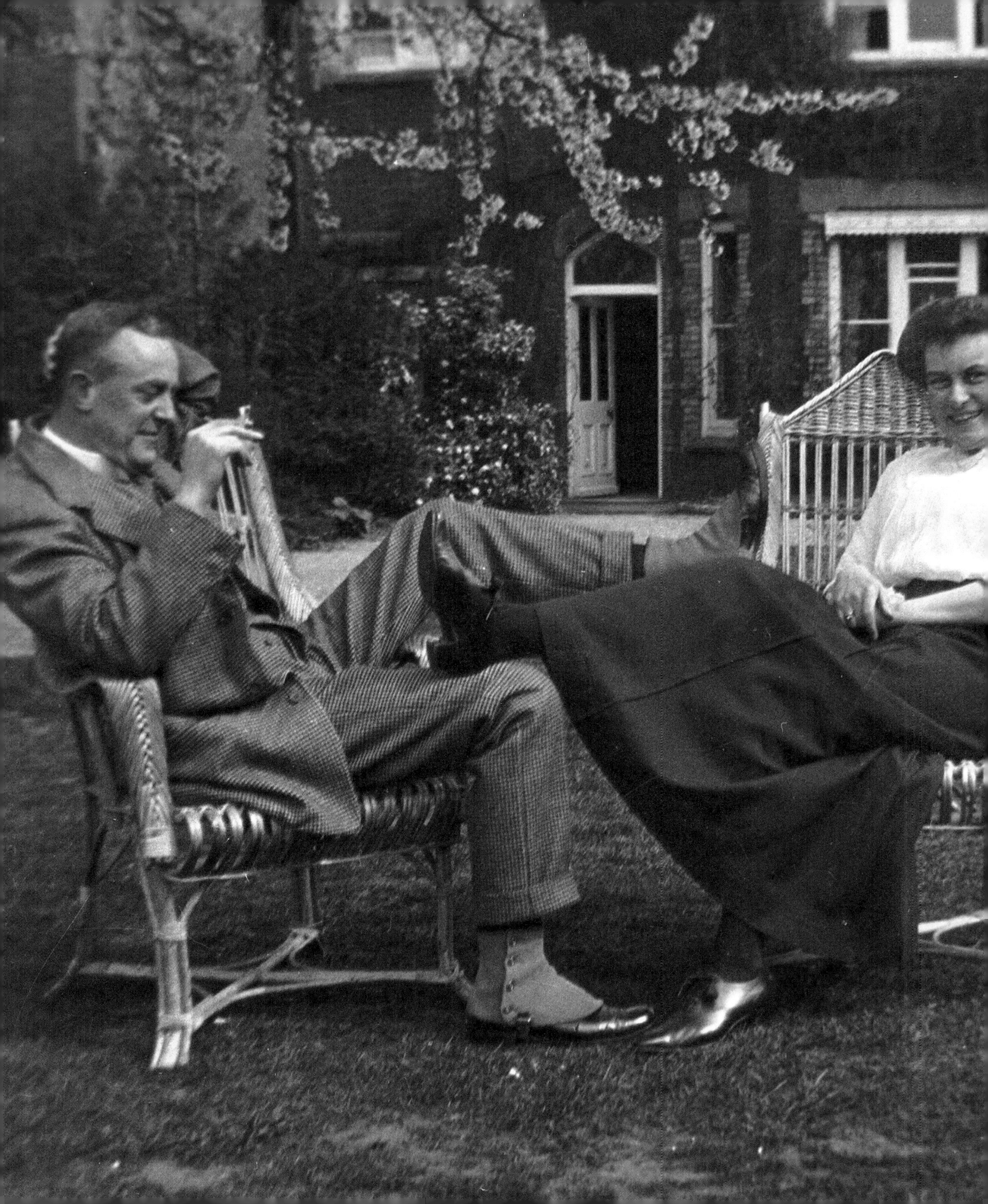

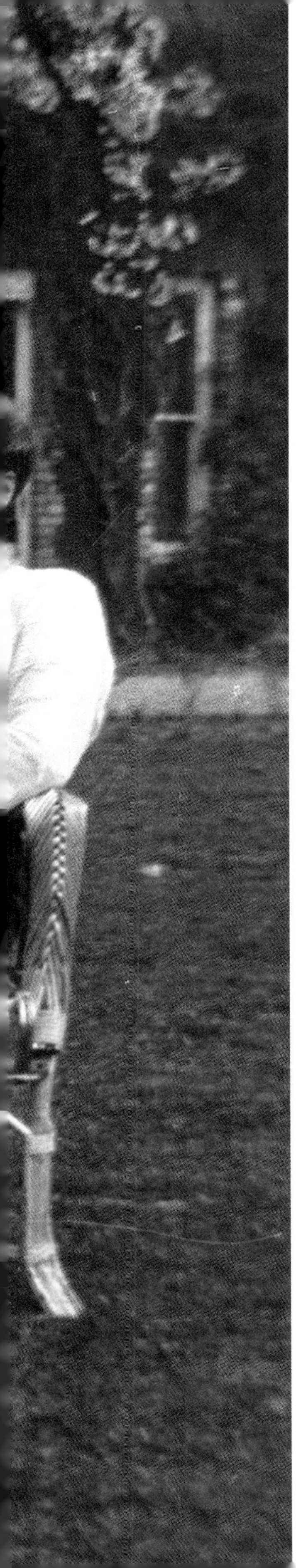

Eleanor Fortescue-Brickdale and Byam Shaw, 1911/12. © Nancy Anderson and John Peele

Introduction

Eleanor Fortescue-Brickdale (1872–1945) was an accomplished painter, illustrator and designer whose artistic life bridged the Victorian and modern worlds. Her work was much influenced by the Pre-Raphaelite artists whose love of detail, colour, symbolism, storytelling and nature was so hugely influential on mid Victorian Britain. Eleanor's own work carried the Pre-Raphaelite style forward into the 20th century. Indeed she became known as 'the last Pre-Raphaelite'.

Like many women of her social class and time – she was born into a financially comfortable household – Eleanor would have been expected to draw and paint in an amateur capacity. By the age of 17 her artistic training became more formal when she had entered the Crystal Palace School of Art. This was followed by stints at the St John's Wood School and then the Royal Academy Schools. At the same time, Eleanor had already begun to produce illustrations for publications such as the *Pall Mall Magazine* and was so successful that she was able to use the profits from her work to pay for her art training. As she became established as an artist she was lucky to have not only the support of her immediate family but also the contacts provided by their social circle. The latter was incredibly important in providing sources of patronage, an especially challenging area for women artists who perhaps did not have the same contacts or opportunities for networking as their male counterparts.

By the end of the 1890s, Eleanor was a successful and well-known artist. Her work struck a chord with the new middle classes – the lawyers, businessmen, clergy, writers, politicians, and philanthropists – who had an interest in culture and the disposable income to buy art. They appreciated her highly detailed, colourful illustrations of the English countryside and her interest in historical narrative. They also admired her use of literary sources, especially Tennyson and Shakespeare. Images of knights, damsels, and peasants appealed to a public fascinated by the romance of the Middle Ages. More symbolic images representing moods and ideas influenced by the work of George Frederick Watts were equally popular. All in all her work empathised with a traditionalism, heroism and patriotism that was still very much in favour up until the Great War.

Reviewers saw connections between Eleanor's work and that of John Byam Liston Shaw (1872–1919), the protégé of John Everett Millais. Indeed the two artists became good friends and when in 1910 Byam Shaw set up a new art school with Vicat Cole, Eleanor was asked to be in charge of watercolour teaching. The early

20th century also saw Eleanor expand her artistic range to include designs for stained glass windows, therefore following the tradition of so many Pre-Raphaelite artists who ventured into the field of applied arts. At her death she was described as the 'last survivor of the Pre-Raphaelite painters'.

Despite her huge popularity in her own time, Eleanor's work has been neglected since her death in 1945. This book, published to coincide with an exhibition on Eleanor's work at the Lady Lever Art Gallery, is the first monograph on the artist. It is the result of extensive research by Pamela Gerrish Nunn, whose work on Pre-Raphaelite women artists has done so much to re-assess the art history of the Victorian period. Here, the author takes us on a journey through Eleanor's training, career and achievements to re-establish her as an important and fascinating figure in the history of Pre-Raphaelite art.

Sandra Penketh
Director of Art Galleries,
National Museums Liverpool

Acknowledgements

This publication and the exhibition it accompanies owe their existence not only to my own efforts but to the expertise and assistance of many people, whom I am glad to be able to thank here.

At National Museums Liverpool, Laura McCulloch for her initial enthusiasm, Sandra Penketh, Myra Brown, Linda Pittwood and Karen Miller for their hard work and dedication to seeing the project through.

For the financial support which has made all the difference, at the research stage and at the point of realisation: The Paul Mellon Centre for Studies in British Art (London) and the Association of Art Historians.

In research institutions and galleries: Caroline Palmer and John Whitely (Ashmolean Museum), Victoria Osbourne (Birmingham Museum and Art Gallery), Jenny Lund and colleagues (Brighton Museum and Art Gallery), Sheena Stoddard and Julia Carver (Bristol City Art Gallery), Richard Burns (Bury Art Gallery), Judy Lindsay (Central Saint Martin's College of Art and Design), Dave Walker and colleagues (Kensington Central Library), Daniel Robbins (Leighton House Museum), Andrew Potter (Royal Academy library), Hannah Hawkworth (Royal Watercolour Society), Melanie Gardner (Tullie House Museum and Art Gallery); staff at the Birmingham City Library, British Library and Print Room, Croydon Record Office, London Metropolitan Archives, National Art Library, Royal Collection at Windsor Castle, Shrewsbury Record Office, Westminster Library, and Women's Art Library at Goldsmith's University (especially Althea Greenan).

For their own interest in and knowledge of the life and work of Eleanor Fortescue-Brickdale, which has aided immeasurably the development of my own: Nancy Anderson, Professor Timothy Barringer, Sally Davis (whose own research has not received the acknowledgement it deserves), Julia Elton, Dr Jan Marsh, Rachel Rolt, Julian Treuherz, Katie Tyreman, Thelma Winyard; and Monica Brewis, John Chrisstoffels, Abi Fletcher, Chris Gay, Christopher Jordan, Dr Rose Lovell-Smith and Sarah Grimes, Lindsay Nunn, Dr Lara Perry and Murray Williams, who have assisted me in invaluably practical fashion.

For access to works and materials in their keeping, in many cases provided at considerable cost to their own commitments: Rachel Baker and colleagues at St Monica's Home of Rest Bristol, Humphrey Clarke, Andrew Clay and Shirley Murrell, Sir Bernard de Hoghton, Father Kimball and colleagues at St Saviour's House Knowle, Peter Mayer, Sister Jean Raphael and colleagues at All Saints' Convent Oxford, Jane Raven, Nicholas Byam Shaw, Natalie Simpson and colleagues (National Trust), Cathryn Spence, staff at Barnardo's Village Barkingside, and staff at St Edmund's College Cambridge.

Pamela Gerrish Nunn

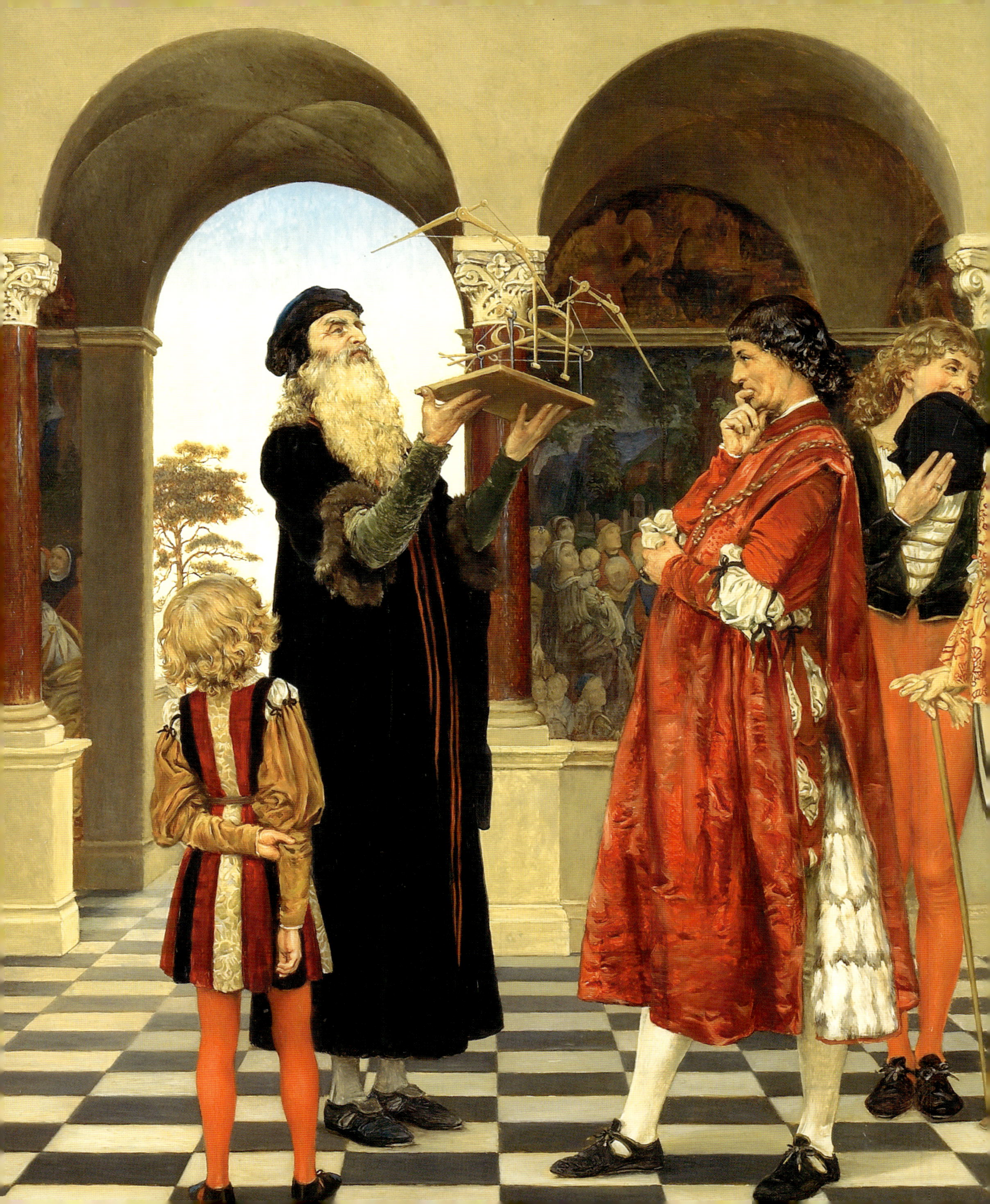

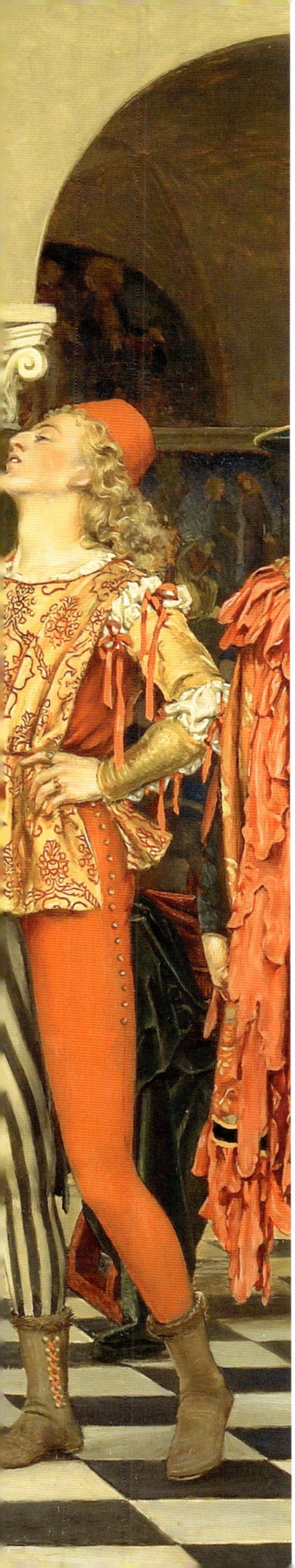

Eleanor Fortescue-Brickdale: A Pre-Raphaelite Journey

Eleanor Fortescue-Brickdale, one of the most popular artists in Britain at the start of the 20th century, was born on 25 January 1872 and died on 10 March 1945, a member of that last generation of Victorians whose lives pivoted on the great divide between the 19th and 20th centuries. Her career as painter, watercolourist and illustrator began in the famous '90s' made notorious by Oscar Wilde, and ended in the melancholy fog of the Second World War. Fortescue-Brickdale can be grouped with many contemporaries of varying reputation: with the late or neo-Pre-Raphaelites who emerged in the wake of Edward Burne-Jones; with the European symbolists who resisted the emergence of Modernism; with the English fairy-painters of the inter-war period who lent enchantment to early 20th-century middle-class childhood. Above all, there are good grounds for locating her output especially as a late expression of the great English style, Pre-Raphaelitism. Begun in the late 1840s and promoted by the authoritative John Ruskin, it swept all before it in mid-Victorian Britain, and was still attracting new recruits in the early 20th century. That Fortescue-Brickdale sensed her life's project was wrapped up in this aesthetic is indicated by a wistful admission in 1927 that she "has been feeling rather 'played out' lately, and feels that Pre-Raphaelitism is no longer wanted".[1] Accordingly, this account of Eleanor Fortescue-Brickdale's life and work considers her career as a journey through the Pre-Raphaelitism she saw herself inheriting, to the point at which its appeal seemed to have evaporated – posited here as the late 1920s, far short as that was of the artist's death in 1945.

Mary Eleanor Fortescue-Brickdale – named for her paternal aunt – was born into a financially comfortable family living in the handsome London suburb of Upper Norwood, where beautiful views over Surrey replaced the inner London surroundings in which the family had lived until a few years previously. She was the last of five children: the oldest, Charles, was 15 years her senior (p. 91), followed by Kate, then John, just two years old at her birth; Anne, born in 1862, had died in 1868. Their father Matthew was a successful barrister who had married a judge's daughter, and when Mary Eleanor was a girl the household included four live-in servants and a governess for her.

This was the kind of family in which the sons were expected to go into the professions, and the daughters to make good marriages. Thus after graduation from Oxford University, Charles followed his father into law and John went into medicine, and over the years both published specialist texts that gave them enduring status in their fields. Neither Kate nor Mary Eleanor ever married, however, and it is tempting to see in this departure from the norms of their class a sign of the changing times, as Victorian Britain became 20th-century Britain, and women finally became citizens. Kate Fortescue-Brickdale remained a private individual, without husband, children, profession, philanthropic causes or scandal to bring her into the public eye, but her younger sister progressed steadily in her chosen field to become one of the most familiar names in Edwardian Britain.

Eleanor's choice of art as a career can be supposed to have begun as a pastime, developed into a vocation and eventually crystallised as an occupation and identity. There are signs that her family was disposed to the arts in a quite specific way, with her father having been a fellow-student of John Ruskin's at Oxford and a founding supporter of the Arundel Society, one of Ruskin's pet projects;[2] and with Charles attending Ruskin's lectures while at university in the 1870s and remaining a keen amateur artist all his life.[3] It can be assumed that the Fortescue-Brickdale home received illustrated periodicals such as the *Cornhill Magazine* and that gallery-going was one of their regular pursuits. Mary Eleanor's own edition of an 1881 re-issue of Lewis Carroll's *Alice in Wonderland*, a present from an aunt and uncle, is coloured in by its enthusiastic young recipient in charming proof of her burgeoning creativity. There are proofs too of a remarkably good eye and hand in ink sketches made on a trip through Germany and Switzerland in 1885, that is to say when she was 13 or 14 years of age, and indications of the ceaseless observer in pencil studies of scenery made in her later teenage years in Surrey, Scotland and elsewhere.

In the mid 1880s the Fortescue-Brickdales moved across the road to a house in a new development described by a late 20th-century commentator as 'later Victorian stockbroker belt',[4] and shortly thereafter Eleanor moved out into the wider world when, at the age of 17 (1889), she enrolled at the nearby Crystal Palace School of Art, Science and Literature.

Although this facility – to call it an institution would be an over-statement – had neither the status of one of the government schools nor the glamour of a school run by a well-known artist, it no doubt had the attraction to the Fortescue-Brickdale parents of lying a few minutes' walk away from the family home. It was based in the Crystal Palace, removed from central London where it had famously housed the Great Exhibition of 1851 and re-erected in south London as a centre for exhibitions, trade shows, entertainment and sundry diversions both didactic and commercial. Young men were admitted to study science and young women to study art, with music welcoming students of both sexes. The chief offering of the school was its vast collection of casts of the 'masterpieces of the antique' and extensive picture gallery boasting 'many admirable specimens of eminent painters who are very poorly represented in the National Gallery'.[5] Though this suggests that the primary opportunity it gave was in art appreciation and copying, Fortescue-Brickdale later gave it credit for providing her with a firm foundation in design.[6] Lectures in anatomy and composition and tuition in 'artistic wood carving' and 'decorative art and design' were among the opportunities offered.[7] Prizes were awarded for drawing from the antique, modelling from the life and from the antique, animal studies, original designs in illustration, oil painting, sculpture and architecture. At the end of the 1890–91 academic year, Fortescue-Brickdale was awarded the annual scholarship for crayon drawing and watercolours, and the following year a silver medal for watercolour.[8]

While Eleanor was attending art school, the now married Charles was living a short walk away with his wife Mabel (née Gibbs) and growing family, while her other brother, John, graduated from Oxford, subsequently moving to Yorkshire to begin his professional life in medicine. To make art her career, Eleanor needed to move on to a more professionally oriented establishment, and at an unknown date in the mid-90s she joined the St John's Wood School. This move may have been both engendered and enabled by the unexpected death of her father in May 1894 (killed in Switzerland while pursuing his favourite pastime of alpinism) and the family's move into central London, though the absence of documentary records for the St John's Wood School makes the date and duration of Fortescue-Brickdale's attendance impossible to pinpoint.

St John's Wood was a stepping-stone to the destination of the Royal Academy (RA) Schools: it was claimed in 1895 that "of the 394 students admitted to the Royal Academy Schools since 1880, we find that 250 were prepared at St John's Wood, and that of 86 prizes awarded by the Royal Academy since 1886, 62 of these were taken by old St John's Wood pupils".[9] Furthermore, all the St John's Wood classes were open equally to women and men students, including study from the nude, which had been for so long denied the aspiring female artist (an inequality remedied at the RA Schools only in 1894). It is likely that here Fortescue-Brickdale first met several eventual colleagues such as Frank Cadogan Cowper.[10]

To aim for the RA Schools at this time looks like a conservative move, given the alternative Slade School in the University of London from which a generation of modern-minded artists was already emerging.[11] It should be borne in mind, however, that the Academy offered free tuition – a factor which, in the absence of any documentary evidence about Fortescue-Brickdale's ambitions, cannot be discounted. In addition, since there were no artists already in the family for Eleanor to follow, it is not surprising if she looked to the mainstream option.

The procedure for entering the RA Schools was to submit certain prescribed pieces of work which secured a person entry as a probationer: if the student proved themselves within the following three months, they would be admitted to a course of study which could last several years. Though Fortescue-Brickdale later related that she had had to make three attempts at attaining probationer standing,[12] once admitted, on 10 January 1895, she proceeded to full studentship within only three weeks. The range of painterly models available to her at the Academy Schools can be surmised from the disparate teaching staff of those years: John Singer Sargent, George Clausen and Arthur Hacker.

Already she had begun to forge a professional practice, a headpiece appearing in the November 1894 issue of the *Pall Mall Magazine* [fig. 1].[13] It was the fashion to inscribe the authorial initials in some discreet corner of the image, and this could eventually bring the black-and-white artist name recognition (p. 46). The risk, one the other hand, was that once the drawing had been sold to the publication it could be used over and over again, obviating the need for further commissions. Thus this vignette was brought out again to head quite another article in the September 1895 issue – but it put an artist's work before a huge audience. When advising young women about the artistic profession much later in life, Fortescue-Brickdale recalled that she was "able almost from the first year to pay the expenses of my own art training. But it involved working very long hours – eg working at black-and-white before going to the school in the morning and also after returning home at night".[14] She advised her readers that "there are chances, which should never be neglected, for a student who is enterprising and has worked hard to gain some commission through open competition – for an advertisement perhaps" – also reflecting her own experience, for it was with such a piece (now untraced) that Fortescue-Brickdale first appeared in exhibition, at the Royal Academy annual show of 1896.[15]

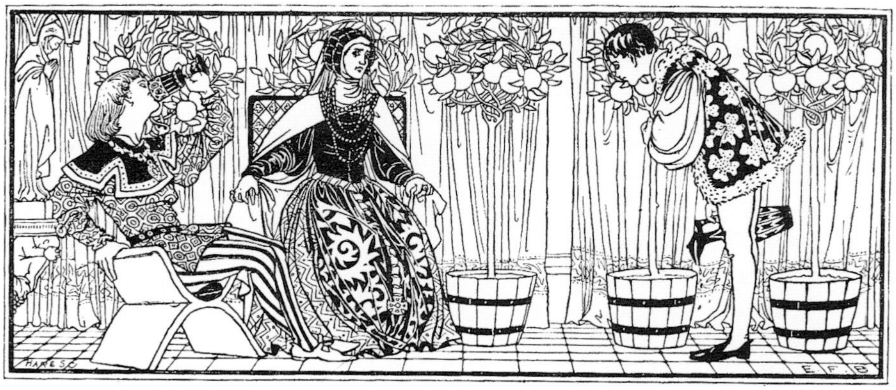

Italian Despots of the Quattro Cento.

IN the midst of the commonplace bustle and wordy circumlocution of these journalistic *fin-de-siècle* days, it is refreshing to the distraught attention to turn to the silence of mediæval times in Italy and pass an hour in the company of that group of brilliant and daring men, the witchery of whose dramatic lives rings like remembered music in our ears. Borgia, Macchiavelli, Sforza, De Medici, Malatesta, Petrucci, Faliero,—what picturesque and thrilling memories these names have power to wake! We can easily portray them, these inimitable cracksmen, despite all the mystifications and misconceptions with which historians have befogged their careers, and trace their fateful hours, their hidden strife, their perilous achievements as readily in the unvarnished records of their era, as we can read their concentrated nature in the furtive, self-contained, sinister portraits of them which Time has spared.

It is true that Victor Hugo and Donizetti and others have done much to render these figures, whether of men or women, morbid or unreal. Cæsar and Lucretia Borgia, in particular, have been represented for two centuries, on the stage and off, as rabid monsters, and it is only in recent years that Gregorovius and Yriarte have patiently tried their lives upon the evidence of fact alone. Macaulay was the first to do justice to the character of Macchiavelli; and it is safe to say that nine-tenths of the crime and vice attributed to the Italian despots originated a century or more after their deaths in the fancy of their biographers. We will take but a single conspicuous instance—that of Lucretia Borgia, wife of Alfonzo d'Este, Duke of Ferrara. The legend which attaches to her name depicts her as a frenzied adultress, using poniard and poison in all directions, and consumed by bursts of tremendous passion. As a matter of fact she never caused or connived at the death of a single human being. On the operatic stage Lucretia dies in a house of ill repute at the climax of a poisoning scene: the truth is that she died in child-bed surrounded by her husband and her children.

The Italian despot has been drawn for us in the ideal by the master-hand of Macchiavelli in his famous essay upon force and fraud—"Il Principe." The Prince, according to this conception, is of necessity a soldier, and as a matter of fact had often risen from the *condottieri*. He should be moderate in self-indulgence, given to physical exercise, of active mind and body, an opulent patron of the Arts, magnificent in hospitality. In point of ethics Macchiavelli is less particular, and expediency is to govern where, in these fastidious days, statesmen might be supposed

Fig. 1
Italian Despots of the Quattrocento, Pall Mall Magazine, 4:19, November 1894, p. 519. University of Canterbury library.

Other early work shows her trying out a variety of ideas that could attract commissions (p. 41). Then at the end of 1897, she was presented to the public as a designer and promising decorative artist by winning one of the annual prizes at the Royal Academy Schools.[16] It was widely reported at the end of the year as a generally poor cohort in which female students shone (the logic connecting those twin verdicts going unexplored!), and Fortescue-Brickdale appeared conspicuous in a roll-call amongst which only Gilbert Bayes and Mary Towgood (later Young Hunter) attained any eventual repute.

Fig. 2

Land Registry certificate, 1898, ink on paper. 41 x 26.5 cm. HM Land Registry.

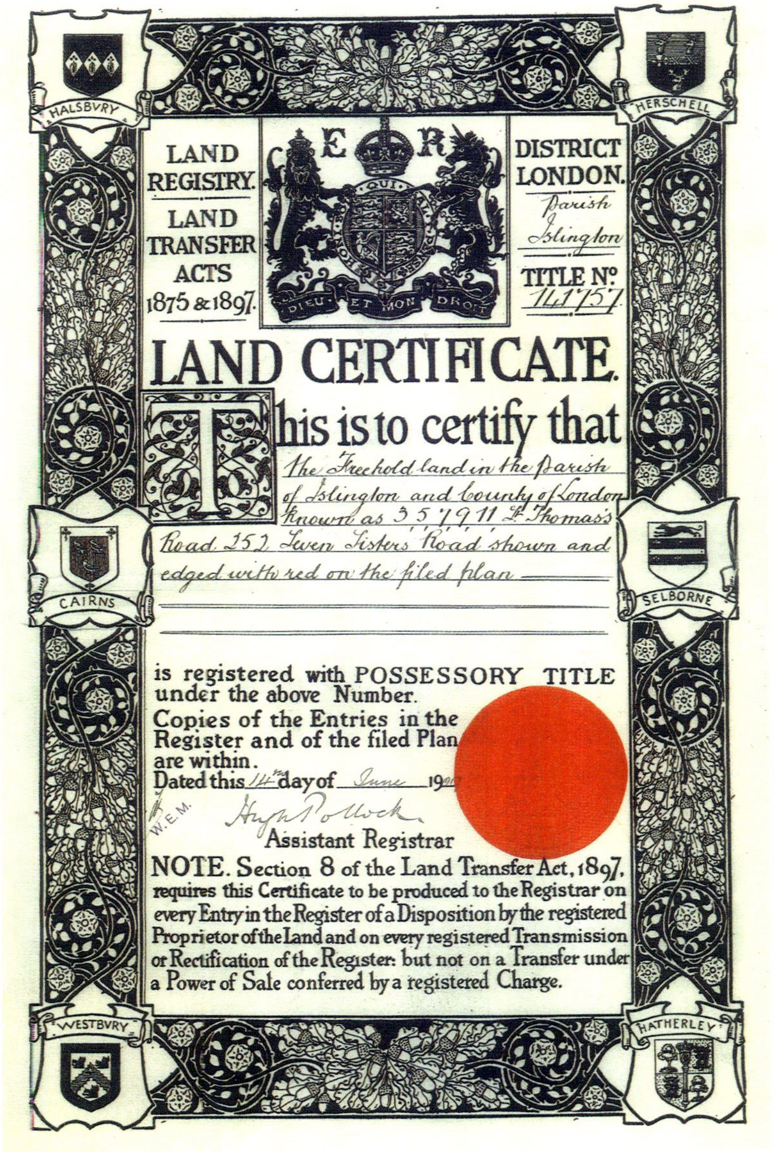
HALSBVRY
HERSCHELL
LAND REGISTRY.
LAND TRANSFER ACTS 1875 & 1897.
E R
DIEU ET MON DROIT
DISTRICT LONDON.
Parish Islington
TITLE No. 141757

LAND CERTIFICATE.

This is to certify that The Freehold land in the Parish of Islington and County of London known as 3 5 7 9 11 St Thomas's Road 257 Seven Sisters' Road shown and edged with red on the filed plan

is registered with POSSESSORY TITLE under the above Number.
Copies of the Entries in the Register and of the filed Plan are within.
Dated this 14th day of June 19
W.E.M. Hugh Pollock
Assistant Registrar

NOTE. Section 8 of the Land Transfer Act, 1897, requires this Certificate to be produced to the Registrar on every Entry in the Register of a Disposition by the registered Proprietor of the Land and on every registered Transmission or Rectification of the Register: but not on a Transfer under a Power of Sale conferred by a registered Charge.

CAIRNS
SELBORNE
WESTBVRY
HATHERLEY

If this prominence was due solely to her own abilities, the momentum that Fortescue-Brickdale's career gathered at this point highlights the other most crucial aspects of any artist's success, patronage. Educated at home and unmarried, she had no public school or university connections to help her through adult life and, along with her art-school acquaintances, family and friends had to be her passport to the world of paid work. In her generation there were innumerable women with an artistic talent who ultimately gained no reputation: but Eleanor Fortescue-Brickdale became one of the most visible artists of her time. For this novice artist – a young, single woman without an artistic inheritance – the significance of the social network into which she was born and in which she moved throughout her life cannot be underestimated. Not only did it help in realising her career but, moreover, it shaped it.

The following year, then, not only did Charles recruit his sister to design a certificate of registration for his newly established Land Registry Office [fig. 2], but she was featured in her brother-in-law J Arthur Gibbs' book *A Cotswold Village* with 20 pen-and-ink sketches of rural scenes described in the text.[17] Gibbs was a friend of Edwin Austin Abbey, the hugely popular American illustrator who was a leading light at the RA at that time, and Abbey himself was known for putting opportunities in the way of his students whenever he could.[18] Again and again in Fortescue-Brickdale's career, the source of an opportunity originated from the sector of society in which she grew up: well-to-do men in the law and their wives; professional, church-going families resident in the Norwood/Crystal Palace area towards the end of the century or in Kensington at the beginning of the 20th; the sons and daughters of life peers stoking the engine of Imperial Britain; landed families with newly acquired country seats and houses in town that needed delineating, decorating and hanging with pictures.

This was not a milieu of inherited titles, lives at court and traditional Tory prejudices, and Fortescue-Brickdale's work attracted such up-to-date people as Liberal MPs, Christian Socialists, suffragists, actors, and pioneers of the aeroplane and automobile industry. Her supporters were the meritocracy that was liberalising Greater Britain – lawyers, politicians, clergymen, writers, publishers, businessmen and philanthropists – people with a public as well as a private life, with disposable incomes and cultivated taste. Fortescue-Brickdale's work, eschewing the modernism of Bloomsbury,[19] endorsed established heroes such as Tennyson and Ruskin, pleasing a clientele that possessed nostalgia for the culture of Christian idealism and a continued belief in an improving art of patriotic optimism.

The Fortescue-Brickdales, the Gibbs and their friends were in microcosm the readership of the new large-format upper-class weeklies *Country Life* and *The Ladies' Field*, begun by George Newnes in January 1897 and March 1898 respectively. The former, focussed on the landed upper class, has been described as "the manual of gentrification for the late Victorian and Edwardian middle classes",[20] part of the liberal trend for appreciation of the English country life and rural traditions that embraced enthusiasm for Helen Allingham's cottage portraiture, the establishment of the National Trust, and the success of gardening guru Gertrude Jekyll. Fortescue-Brickdale's charming and varied designs for these titles [fig. 3] allowed her to work out a repertoire that she was able to develop and mine for years to come. [21] They sat alongside contributions by her friend John Byam Shaw and others such as Arthur Rackham, Harold Nelson and Miriam Garden and, after her first appearance in January 1898, not an issue of *Country Life* appeared without something from Fortescue-Brickdale's hand until January 1909.[22] Whether for regular columns on books, farming topics and readers' letters or for one-off articles and stories, her designs drew her to the attention of an audience from which she was to draw numerous patrons in the process of her long career. This sector of society was also a steady source of commissions for portraits and, with its big houses in extensive grounds and historic settings, handily facilitated Fortescue-Brickdale's growing need for historic, decorative and natural backgrounds for her watercolours and paintings (pp. 63, 69).[23]Another opportunity offered by this class was in the *fin-de-siècle* fashion for book-plates, which gave black-and-white artists another string to their bow. [24] It is telling of her progress that by the end of 1898, Fortescue-Brickdale was keeping a notebook of sales achieved.[25]

Though she lacked the status that would have put her name on the frontispiece of *A Cotswold Village*, the next book the promising newcomer was commissioned to illustrate recognised her as a coming black-and-white artist with audience appeal. The ten drawings that Fortescue-Brickdale contributed to Walter Scott's well-known medievalist adventure in Bell and Sons' illustrated edition of *Ivanhoe* that came out in 1900 made her familiarity with the Pre-Raphaelite repertoire more obvious.[26] Meant for use in schools, this was a cheap and cheerful publication, but once again put the artist's name before a huge audience as the colleague of Bell's other illustrators, who included Byam Shaw and Robert Anning Bell. She progressed to colour illustration with a share of the Constable edition of Shakespeare's works (p. 45) published in 1901, which put her into the company of Shaw, Cadogan Cowper, Gerald Moira and others.

The first published article on Fortescue-Brickdale, in March 1898, had labelled her a designer and illustrator,[27] and it could be said that less than two years later she was not only well on the way to establishing herself as such but also making strong claims as a painter, with oils shown at the annual RA exhibitions. Her first, at the 1899 exhibition, *The pale Complexion of True Love,* advertised her admiration for Edwin Austin Abbey, but as the new century opened she made it emphatically clear that she had her own ideas, exhibiting not only literary

Fig. 3

Royal Dublin Horse Show. *The Ladies' Field*, 3 September 1898, p. 557. St Peter's House Library, University of Brighton.

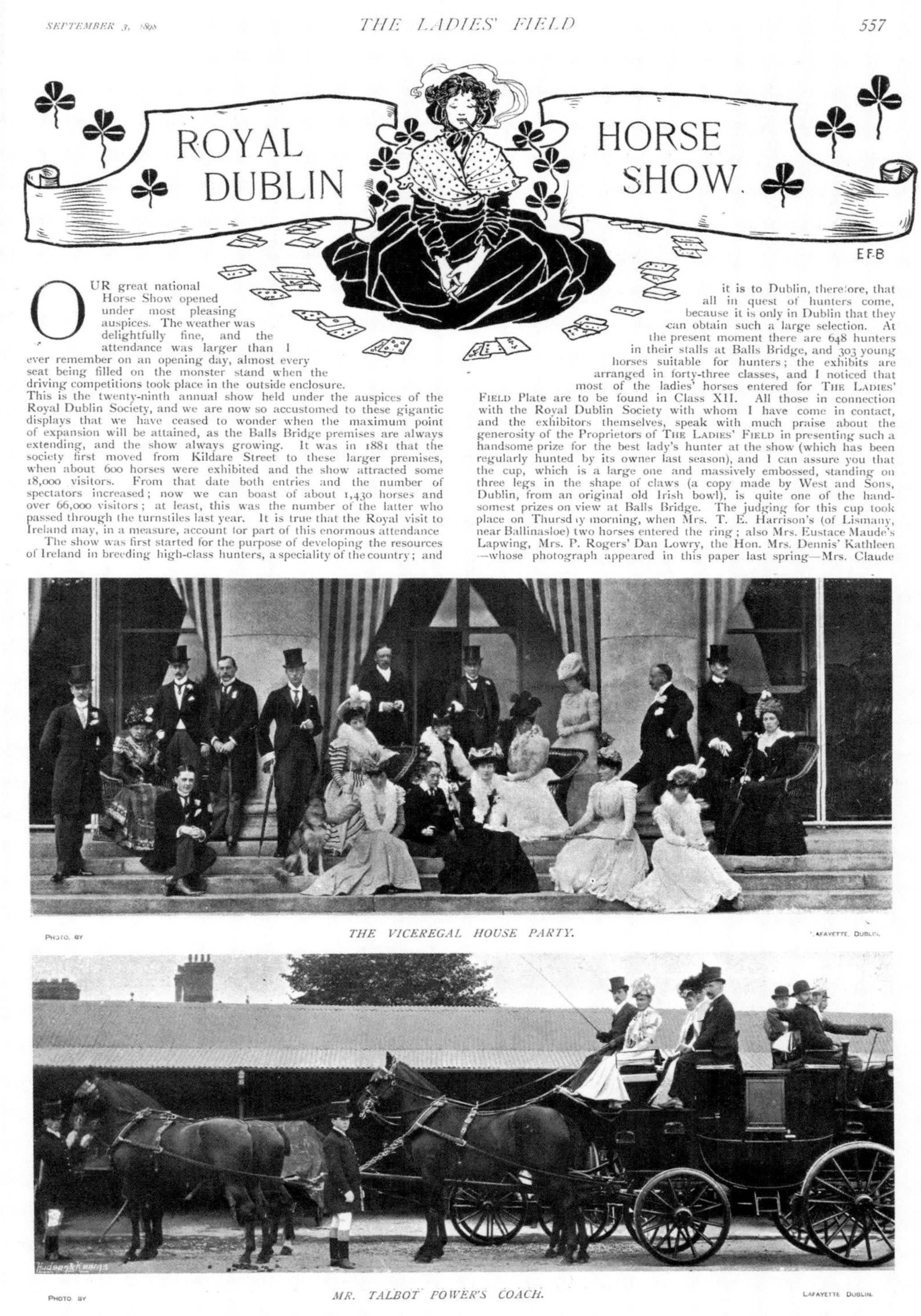

SEPTEMBER 3, 1898 THE LADIES' FIELD 557

ROYAL DUBLIN HORSE SHOW.

EFB

OUR great national Horse Show opened under most pleasing auspices. The weather was delightfully fine, and the attendance was larger than I ever remember on an opening day, almost every seat being filled on the monster stand when the driving competitions took place in the outside enclosure. This is the twenty-ninth annual show held under the auspices of the Royal Dublin Society, and we are now so accustomed to these gigantic displays that we have ceased to wonder when the maximum point of expansion will be attained, as the Balls Bridge premises are always extending, and the show always growing. It was in 1881 that the society first moved from Kildare Street to these larger premises, when about 600 horses were exhibited and the show attracted some 18,000 visitors. From that date both entries and the number of spectators increased; now we can boast of about 1,430 horses and over 66,000 visitors; at least, this was the number of the latter who passed through the turnstiles last year. It is true that the Royal visit to Ireland may, in a measure, account for part of this enormous attendance

The show was first started for the purpose of developing the resources of Ireland in breeding high-class hunters, a speciality of the country; and it is to Dublin, therefore, that all in quest of hunters come, because it is only in Dublin that they can obtain such a large selection. At the present moment there are 648 hunters in their stalls at Balls Bridge, and 303 young horses suitable for hunters; the exhibits are arranged in forty-three classes, and I noticed that most of the ladies' horses entered for THE LADIES' FIELD Plate are to be found in Class XII. All those in connection with the Royal Dublin Society with whom I have come in contact, and the exhibitors themselves, speak with much praise about the generosity of the Proprietors of THE LADIES' FIELD in presenting such a handsome prize for the best lady's hunter at the show (which has been regularly hunted by its owner last season), and I can assure you that the cup, which is a large one and massively embossed, standing on three legs in the shape of claws (a copy made by West and Sons, Dublin, from an original old Irish bowl), is quite one of the handsomest prizes on view at Balls Bridge. The judging for this cup took place on Thursday morning, when Mrs. T. E. Harrison's (of Lismany, near Ballinasloe) two horses entered the ring; also Mrs. Eustace Maude's Lapwing, Mrs. P. Rogers' Dan Lowry, the Hon. Mrs. Dennis' Kathleen—whose photograph appeared in this paper last spring—Mrs. Claude

PHOTO. BY THE VICEREGAL HOUSE PARTY. LAFAYETTE, DUBLIN.

PHOTO. BY MR. TALBOT POWER'S COACH. LAFAYETTE, DUBLIN.

subjects [figs. 4, 5] but original scenes addressing the abstract concepts that George Frederick Watts, above all, had promoted to the late-Victorian public. The titles of Fortescue-Brickdale's exhibits over the next five years indicate a deep investment in these symbolic concepts, which the millennium made particularly timely: *Time and the Maiden* (1899), *Time the Physician* (1900) (p. 42), *The Deceitfulness of Riches* (1901), *Justice before her Judge* (1902), *Love and his Counterfeits* (1904) established her as an allegorist seeking to make decorative parables.[28] As a girl, she was unlikely to have learnt Latin and Greek, or read Plato and Kant, but her reading in English literature was probably wide-ranging. With that mental furniture, she populated her paintings with several elements common at the time: historically costumed figures against historical architecture; winged figures of indeterminate sex presumed to be angels or cupids; symbolic male and female figures; peasants, infants, knights and ladies. In this vocabulary, as in that of its principal begetter, Burne-Jones, contemporary subject-matter played but a minor part.

As a painter, though, Fortescue-Brickdale was diverted into watercolour by her next big opportunity and, while this made her name, it located her within the secondary rank of painters, since oil was still accepted as the primary medium for painting (though watercolour may have been more viable for many artists). This positioning of her practice came about through the commission in summer 1899 from the art dealers Dowdeswell's for a show of watercolours that came to fruition in June 1901 under the Shakespearean title 'Such stuff as dreams are made of!' Subject-matter included the Wattsian abstracts she had already essayed in oil, romantic anecdote, 'fancy pictures' and poetic moralities, with titles drawn from the Bible [fig. 5], Shakespeare and other literary favourites including Robert Browning, Christina Rossetti and Coleridge. Complex, interlocking spaces and a love of pattern, detailed costuming and vivid jewel-like colour characterised these works.

It may have been this commission that promoted Fortescue-Brickdale's acquisition of her own studio, in the west London area of Holland Park where so many other artists lived and worked,[29] and it was spectacularly successful, with the press gushing with talk of overnight success, and all 45 exhibits said to be sold.[30] Critics linked Fortescue-Brickdale definitively with Pre-Raphaelitism which, though born half a century before, was kept alive not least by the fact that Arthur Hughes and William Holman Hunt were still active.[31] To which of the Pre-Raphaelite artists Fortescue-Brickdale owed most was a matter of opinion, some pointing to John Everett Millais and Hunt, some to Dante Gabriel Rossetti and Burne-Jones, others to Ford Madox Brown. Though not exactly topical, these artists commanded tremendous respect at the beginning of the 20th century, so to be connected with them was a compliment rather than a put-down. The success of Burne-Jones, in particular, only recently deceased (1898), fired numerous painters in these first years of the 20th century.[32]

The extravagant flavour of the press Fortescue-Brickdale's show attracted can be ably demonstrated by the remarks made in *The Artist*'s review, accompanied by illustrations of four of the exhibits:

> "Rarely, if ever, has a woman painter made a great reputation as quickly and thoroughly as Miss Eleanor Fortescue-Brickdale, whose series of watercolour drawings has, during the last month, drawn the whole of artistic London to the Dowdeswell Galleries. Since cut flowers have ceased to monopolise the attention of women painters, they have, to a large extent, taken up impressionism of the worst type... It is the contrast between Miss Brickdale's work and that of other women-painters that gives full significance to the manifestation of Miss Brickdale's exceptional talent. She combines great

> technical skill with an extremely felicitous, quaint imagination and rare poetic feeling... [This exhibition] should be sufficient to secure her a leading position among the women artists of this country."[33]

While not all commentators clung to this old-fashioned categorisation of female artists by gender, this way of thinking was dear to some of those who waxed most enthusiastic in Fortescue-Brickdale's praise, such as Walter Shaw Sparrow, who wrote for *The Studio* and would soon illustrate his segregationist thesis with the compendious *Women Painters of the World* (1905).[34] This opinion of Fortescue-Brickdale's work reflects more ideology than reason, since her work was simultaneously accused of resembling too closely that of her male colleague, Byam Shaw,[35] as well as drawing on the work of the male artists of Pre-Raphaelitism. In fact her imagery was much more various and drawn from much broader a spectrum than was habitually allowed in 'woman's sphere' – which meant domestic incident, children, women and girls as subjects, and heterosexual romance as a primary theme, with a preference for the light, the lachrymose and sentimental. Fortescue-Brickdale had already shown equal use of male protagonists and female, did not feel constrained to place her subjects within the home or family, and did not promote a gendered distribution of moral or personal characteristics (p. 42). Whatever her own views, however,[36] she will have been aware that etiquette and prejudice still expected women to distinguish themselves from men in traditional ways.

Another response provoked by this first solo show took up the question of illustration versus imaginative art. Where, some reviewers asked, did the illustrator end and the artist begin? Was Fortescue-Brickdale, an evidently talented illustrator, capable of interpretation, or, better, invention? Could she satisfy Ruskin's view of the matter that "you never can have illustrations of poetry; you only have the thoughts which occur to another original mind in reading the verse"?[37] She will have appreciated that the credible artist – even more than the designer – must be as much an inventor as a delineator, offering the viewer personal vision as well as technical excellence. This matter continued to be raised, and, in the long term, Fortescue-Brickdale may have suffered like many other women artists had before her and continued to do – despite very real changes in their situation occurring during her lifetime – from a combination of limited education, constrained worldly experience and excessive trust in the men around her. Though she was admired by Watts,[38] Fortescue-Brickdale was surrounded by second-rank or minor artists, some of whom remained close to her throughout her entire working life. None of the leading female artists of the Edwardian period (Evelyn DeMorgan, Elizabeth Forbes, Marianne Stokes, Lucy Kemp-Welch, Annie Swynnerton, Laura Knight) nor the artists seen then as pioneers of modern art (Walter Sickert, Augustus John, William Orpen, Vanessa Bell) figured amongst her friends.

For the moment, however, Fortescue-Brickdale's star was definitely in the ascendant. Her one-woman show began a period of intense visibility such that, over the next few years, her name seemed to be everywhere. Long articles on her appeared in a variety of periodicals, encouraged by a reprise of her solo show in February 1902 at Leighton House, Kensington, and the contemporaneous exhibition at the 1902 Pastel Society show of a full-length portrait of her by Shaw.[39] Writer Edith Sichel, sent to interview Fortescue-Brickdale in 1901, reported to a friend in South Africa, "She is a new painter, a really inspired force, exquisite in colour and poetic idea. I don't think I have had so much pleasure from a modern [sic] since the Pre-Raphaelites, but she is not like them in an imitative way. I went to see her before coming away – an interesting girl of twenty-six, cultivated and calm, with all the calm of real gift. She not only possesses her soul, but she has a soul to possess. [My dear friend] Mary has gone quite wild about her."[40] Similarly, the

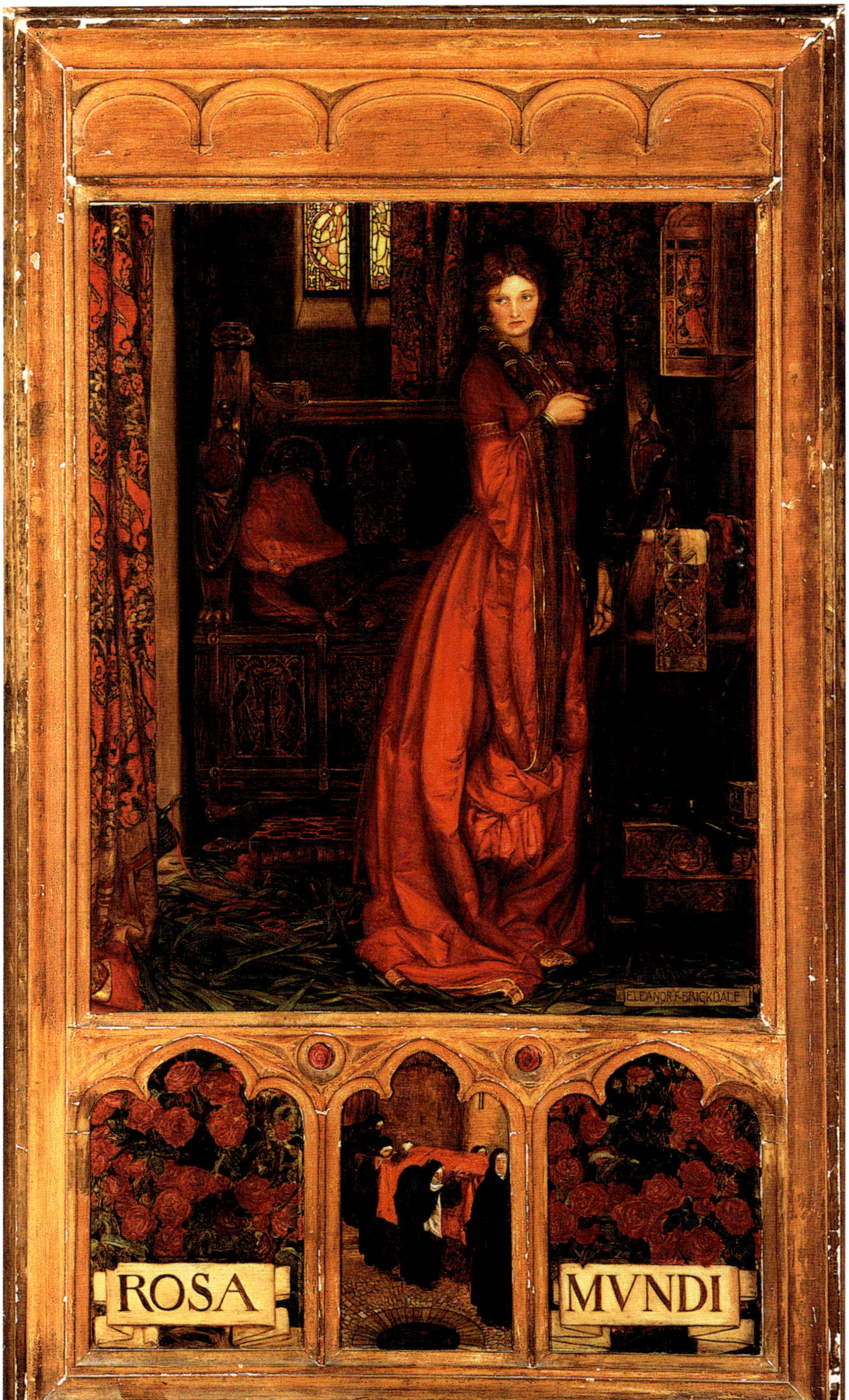

Fig. 4
Rosamond, 1903, oil.
122 x 73.5 cm. Courtesy of
Sotheby's Picture Library.

New Zealand painter Frances Hodgkins wrote home from London in 1902, "...we hied West to Leighton House there to see Miss Eleanor Brickdale's pictures. They were beautiful - about 40 smallish sized watercolours - illustrating allegories and proverbs treated decoratively... colour flashed jewel-like from every frame - oh! happy woman to paint like that and give such pleasure - it was a refreshment of the soul to see them...and London is raving over her".[41] Meanwhile, under the heading "The new Development in English Art", half a world away Hodgkins' compatriots were told, "Strangely enough the newest developments of painting [are] on the lines adopted in the early fifties by Rossetti and his friends. It is Miss Eleanor Brickdale and Mr Byam Shaw whom those most keenly interested in art regard as the two coming artists of the English school ... [T]heir pictures and their personalities are among the most interesting pictures and the most interesting art personalities of the day".[42] In proof of this standing, she was elected to the Society of Oil Painters and extended her exhibition appearances to include the Royal Society of Watercolour Painters - the venue to which she became more attached than any other in the long term - and in the Academy exhibition of 1903, Fortescue-Brickdale's *Rosamond* [fig. 4] was hung on the line, "given the place of honour" amongst "the followers of the Pre-Raphaelites" while she was chosen to exemplify neo-Pre-Raphaelitism in *The Studio* publication of that year *Representative Art of our Time*.[43] These alliances settled her in territory defined by *The Times* as old-fashioned but

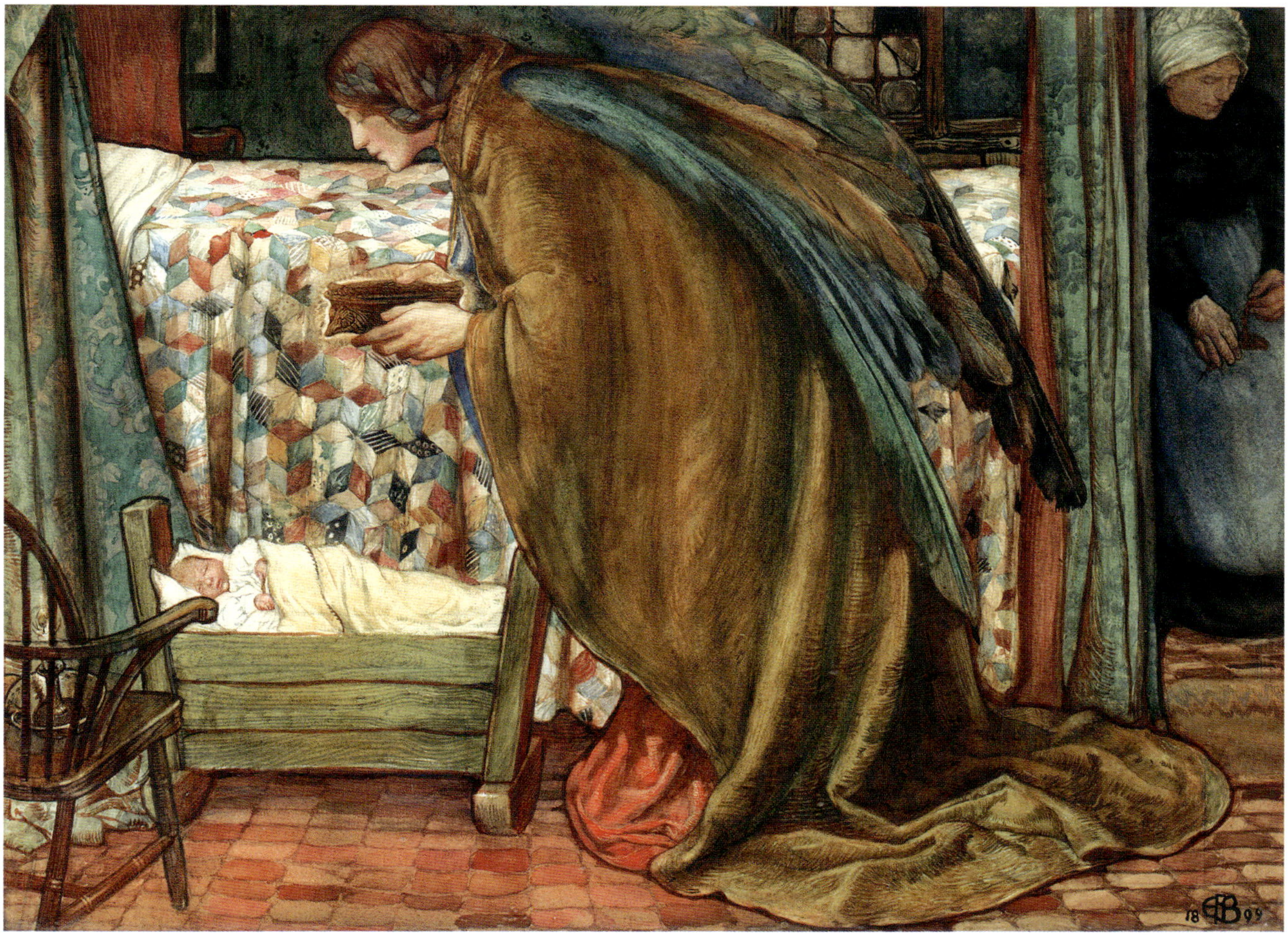

Fig. 5
The Gift that is better than Rubies, 1899, watercolour and bodycolour. 34 x 47 cm. Courtesy of Sotheby's Picture Library.

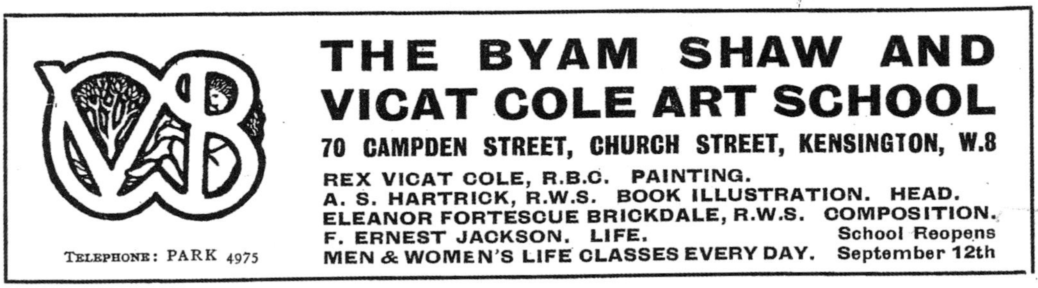

Fig. 6
Advertisement, *The Studio*, 83: 346, January 1922, p. xi. Central Saint Martins College of Art and Design, Museum and Study Collection.

commanding 'the balance of favour on the part of the picture-seeing public'.[44]

While such subjects as Rosamond trailed an unmistakably Pre-Raphaelite pedigree (Fortescue-Brickdale's version harking back to Millais' famous *Mariana*, 1851), it was agreed by critics and public alike that, beyond this, Fortescue-Brickdale presented, in Sparrow's words, "a most blessed companionship of high thoughts and right feelings",[45] though provoking some irritation with the opacity of her messages. The symbolism of the original Pre-Raphaelites, however, had been found arcane or perverse, while Watts' idiosyncratic rewriting of the canon had not harmed his standing, and his death in 1904 probably prompted such a work as *Labour and the broken Heart*, 1904–5, (p. 49), one of the many allegories and parables on display in Brickdale's second solo show for Dowdeswell's in June 1905.[46] Another influence was her friend Shaw's pursuit of symbolic allegory. The closeness between these two led some to assume she was under his sway, and certainly some ideas occurring in both artists' works at this time, such as bound and tied women, seem unlikely inventions on her part.[47] Though Fortescue-Brickdale baffled many viewers with motifs of her own devising at the RA and the Royal Watercolour Society (RWS), compositions such as *The Three Daughters of Time* (1902), *Illusion's Burial* (1903) and *Scandal* (1904) were only attracting the kind of exasperation that the original Pre-Raphaelites, Watts and Shaw had in turn provoked.

The Pre-Raphaelite connection was echoed further in a black-and-white illustrated edition of Tennyson's poems that Fortescue-Brickdale produced for Bell's in 1905.[48] There was no cessation in admiration for Tennyson and the Arthurian legacy he had so effectively appropriated, and Brickdale will have been aware of Stopford Brooke's *Tennyson, his art and relation to modern life* and the numerous stage versions of Arthurian subjects that appeared steadily during the turn of the century.[49] But, as George Layard's 1894 publication *Tennyson and his Pre-Raphaelite Illustrators* had made clear, the late Poet Laureate had provided the motif for so many of the Pre-Raphaelites' most successful works that this suite of 70 drawings put Brickdale into direct comparison with the founding Pre-Raphaelites.[50] Her task was to reinforce the reader's belief in the validity of Tennyson's characters and stories without merely reiterating what earlier artists had seen in them. Such subjects as Mariana, Oriana, The Lady of Shalott, The Gardener's Daughter, Locksley Hall, St Agnes' Eve and The talking Oak were bound to recall for the well-informed viewer works from almost half a century earlier by Millais, Hunt, Sandys, Rossetti, Hughes and Cameron, despite the absence of the colour which had been a primary element of original Pre-Raphaelitism. As C Lewis Hind wrote at this time in respect of Frederick Cayley Robinson, "We are none of us original. The fingers of the great ones of the past are always stretching dimly out and pressing our brains. All we can expect is that a time may come in our lives when, having passed from the more active influences of the Masters who have formed us, we 'find ourselves' and add our spark of originality to the glowing fire", naming Fortescue-Brickdale in a list of contemporary artists practising the same 'symbolistic, inward-brooding' work as his subject.[51]

At the same time, the potential depth of Fortescue-Brickdale's art was developed by designing for the fashionable firm of 'art-manufacturers' Liberty,[52] and her exhibition at The Leicester Galleries in late 1904 of a richly coloured and patterned statuette, *The Chatelaine* – a "medium which she eventually intends to give fuller attention to".[53] This impressive work evoked not only the tastes of the New sculptors[54] but the Chaucerian strand of the Pre-Raphaelite repertoire. And as she proceeded, Fortescue-Brickdale's range of literary sources became ever wider, with her 1905 show at Dowdeswell's rich with references to the poetry of Browning and William Morris; Biblical illustrations to Mabel Dearmer's *A Child's Life of Christ* in 1906;[55] and subjects from old English balladry in *The little Foot-Page* (1905) (p. 50) and *Following the Queen of the Gypsies oh* (1905). This almost constant visibility secured Fortescue-Brickdale's place in the public's mind alongside Walter Crane, Byam Shaw, Robert Anning Bell and Arthur Rackham as one of the artists who were making neo-Pre-Raphaelite illustration, decoration and painting popular cultural forms of the early 20th century.

As illustrators, these artists often received commissions from different publishers for the same literary works or authors, emphasising the richness of the field by direct competition. Fortescue-Brickdale was by no means the only woman in the frame: not only did the well-known Elizabeth Forbes bring out *King Arthur's Wood* in 1904, but others such as Jessie Marion King (*The Defence of Guinevere and other poems*, 1904), Florence Harrison (*In the Fairy Ring*, 1908) and Gertrude Demain Hammond (*Stories from Shakespeare*, 1910) worked this territory, albeit with less stylistic affiliation to Pre-Raphaelitism.[56] More often than not, this kind of work meant treading in the footsteps of other artists –

Fig. 7
Saints Francis, Helen and Clare, St Saviour's House (formerly Convent of the Sisters of Charity), Knowle, 1914.

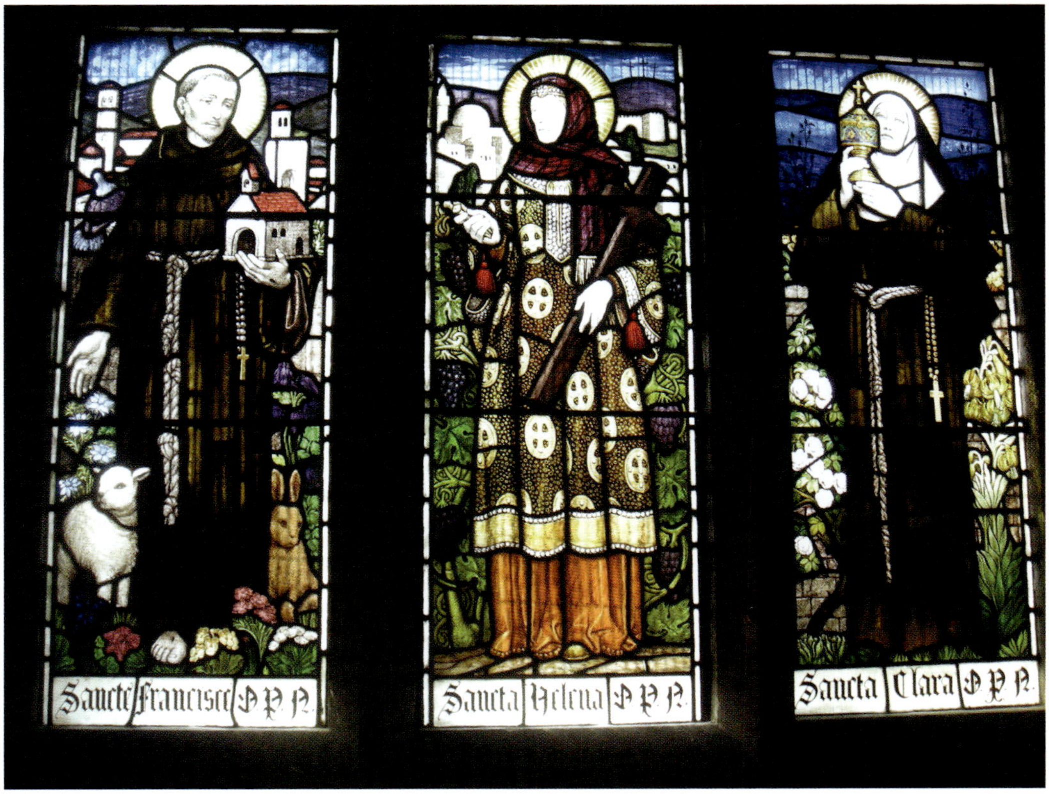

an irksome situation for most artists and especially disadvantageous for women, whom it was customary to evaluate by invidious comparison. Given the mixed reception of Fortescue-Brickdale's illustration of the works of Robert Browning (published December 1908 and December 1909, exhibition May–July 1909) (pp. 56, 59)[57], it is worth noting that the teaming up of authors with artists is difficult to evaluate now without detailed documentation from publishers, artists and authors, which does not survive in many cases; and it is irresistible to speculate whether Brickdale was ever offered the poetry of Malory, Wordsworth, Elizabeth Barrett Browning or Christina Rossetti to illustrate. Further, it is hard not to regret that she was apparently given so little opportunity to develop a contemporary vision, which is glimpsed only here and there in her literary treatments (pp. 60, 74).

That said, the variety in Fortescue-Brickdale's creative practice continued to develop, indicating that she still saw herself as an artist who was as much a designer as a painter. In the summer of 1907, she was drawn by her friend Dion Clayton Calthrop into the fashion for pageants,[58] while a further dimension of her skills in two-dimensional work was made clear in 12 watercolours in the Wright Brothers' 17-part *Beautiful Flowers and how to grow Them*, appearing during 1909 (p. 61). This gave rise in turn to the issuing of a flower calendar of Fortescue-Brickdale's designs, complimented for combining accuracy with pictorial charm and aesthetic merit.[59] Of course, the Pre-Raphaelite in her venerated nature and its myriad forms, observed them closely and believed in nature's value for the spirituality and morality of humankind but, even though this had been visible in such works as *The little Foot-Page* (p. 51), it was not until the Wright publication that this artist's sympathetic skill in the delineation of nature – somehow the expression 'still life' seems inadequate – was so gracefully exposed.[60]

This was a key element of the suite of watercolours commissioned in 1909 by her new dealer Ernest Brown, who ran The Leicester Galleries, and published in Hodder and Stoughton's illustrated editions of Tennyson's *Idylls of the King* (pp. 64–69), which appeared in 1911. The initial commission, probably provoked by the centenary of the poet's birth, asked for 28 drawings, though the books (a deluxe edition and a popular edition) used only 21 and 12 compositions respectively. Readers, then, saw only the original four Idylls that had appeared in 1859, devoted to the female characters from the Arthurian stories, Enid, Vivien, Elaine, and Guinevere, without the episodes concerning King Arthur and knights Lancelot and Gareth included in exhibition. Explicitly reinforcing for some reviewers the artist's Pre-Raphaelitism and femininity, [61] this sequence of pictures celebrates natural settings and their detail, in the various stages of Geraint and Enid's foolish rambles, in key scenes of Vivien's enslavement of Merlin, in the more sophisticated images of Elaine's sad story, and in the account of the flawed heroine Guinevere. The presence of individualised plants, bushes, grasses and trees gives the magic touch to many of the works that were on exhibition 'alongside Arthur Rackham's latest work' at The Leicester Galleries in October 1911.

This publication was a greater critical success than her Browning designs, which had been seen to fall short of the poet's highly individual, sensual and, it could be said, masculine spirit. Browning's "dubious, self-exculpating, failed, doubting characters from the margins of morality, religion, art, intellect, society, history"[62] may have been alien to Fortescue-Brickdale's psychology, while the version of the Arthurian world that Tennyson offered in the Idylls was generally agreed to be founded on conservative sexual politics invested in the polarisation of good women and bad on whose behaviours the prosperity of their entire society depended. This may – sadly, it could be said – have been more familiar to the artist.[63] In this respect, this project shifted Fortescue-Brickdale's repertoire more toward the *idées reçues* of Tennyson's sexual politics – and the feminine sphere for which admirers such as Sparrow had already tried to claim her. Though, as has already been asserted, Fortescue-Brickdale was capable of much more than this, the femininity of her interpretation of the Idylls is marked in contrast with the vigorous work of, say, Florence Harrison, who illustrated Tennyson's *Guinevere* for Blackie just a year later.[64] Without documentary evidence, though, it is tantalisingly impossible to say how self-determining Fortescue-Brickdale's programme of work was or whether she was steered by others into what conservative taste designated 'women's work'.

No evidence remains of Fortescue-Brickdale's view, in these eventful years in Britain's evolution into a modern society, of the Liberal landslide in the 1906 election, the great demonstrations by the suffragists in 1908, the unrest provoked by Lloyd George's budget in 1909, or the shocking Post-Impressionist exhibitions of 1910 and 1912. Her family life underwent substantial changes at this time, with a move in 1908 to the West Kensington house that would be her and her sister Kate's home for the next 30 years, her mother Sarah's death in 1909, and her brother Charles' knighthood in 1911.

With impressive commitment, Fortescue-Brickdale's regular production of the range of work described so far continued. She even managed to supplement her productivity with a secondary professional life as a teacher. With Byam Shaw, and his great friend Rex Vicat Cole, she had been contributing since 1905 to the teaching programme of the art school of King's College for Women, teaching one morning a week at the Kensington premises: advertisements in autumn 1909 describe the school as being 'under the immediate direction' of these three, with two further artists named as honorary visitors and another pair identified as assistants. By 1910 Cole and Shaw were dissatisfied with it (Cole had started it in 1894, and Shaw had been involved since 1904), and resolved to set up their own art school.[65]

This came about in May 1910, with custom-built premises in Kensington and a teaching staff of whom Shaw and Cole were the joint principals; Fortescue-Brickdale was in charge of Watercolour with a second string in Composition.[66] She it was who designed the school's insignia (what would nowadays be called its logo) [fig. 6], playing on the two men's initials and imagery dear to both her and Shaw. While the extent of her involvement has, curiously, been occluded by the chief accounts of the school,[67] Fortescue-Brickdale's commitment to it is indicated by her support not just at its launch but later, when Shaw unexpectedly died. Though written accounts of her presence at the school may be sparse, her magnificent portrait of student Winifred Roberts (later Nicholson) (p. 70) hints at the intensity of Fortescue-Brickdale's involvement.

She continued to expand her range of artistic output, in 1912 designing a stained glass window for her patrons the Buxtons of Newtimber, near Brighton, the first of many memorial windows she was to design over the next 25 years. There is no evidence that Brickdale ever learnt to work with glass, however, and most of her designs were executed by the firm of Burlison and Grylls, the longest-lasting of the Arts and Crafts glass specialists.[68] Again, the obvious precedent would have lain in Pre-Raphaelitism, with the windows of Morris and Company, especially in its designs by Burne-Jones. The single figure of St Francis in the Buxton window stood her in good stead for her next design, in 1914, [fig. 7] for the house of charity in Bristol founded by her maternal aunt Elizabeth Lloyd, where the vivid figures of saints Francis, Helen and Clare complement the Mater Dolorosa. While piety is not necessary for an artist to make effective devotional works, it can be guessed that such projects spoke to Fortescue-Brickdale's own beliefs, which seem to have sat within High Anglicanism. Thus her illustration of William Canton's *Story of Saint Elizabeth of Hungary* (1912) and Michael Fairless' *Gathering of Brother Hilarius* (1913) may have been labours of love as much as commercial undertakings, while numerous individual compositions of sacred subjects throughout Fortescue-Brickdale's oeuvre, whose genesis is as yet

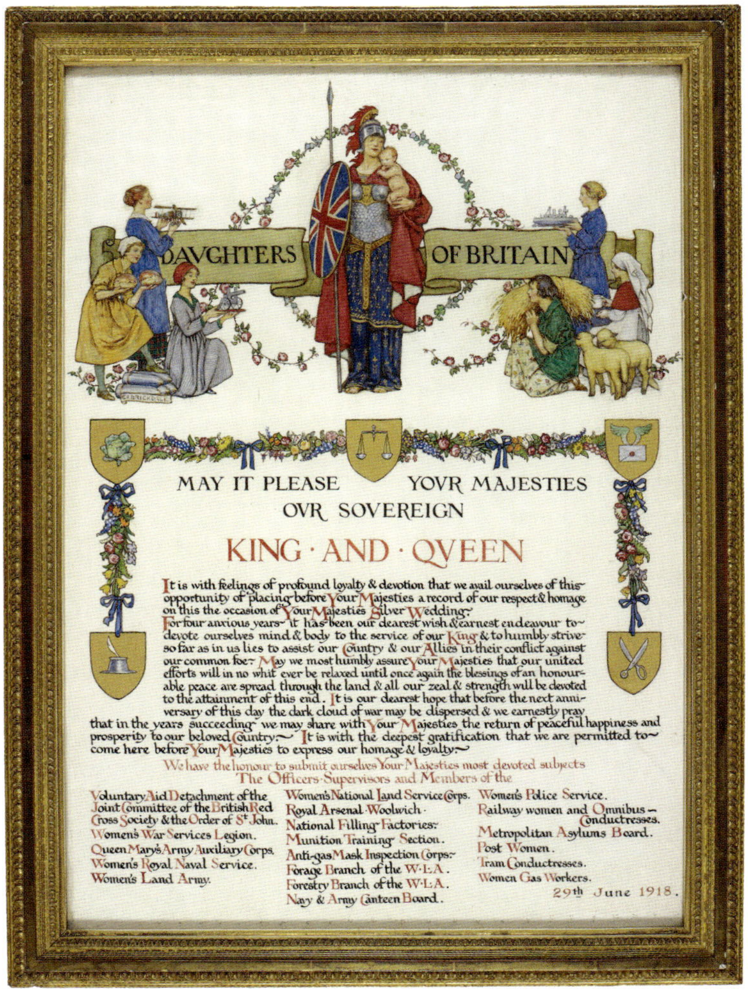

Fig. 8
Address to Her Majesty Queen Mary, 1918, watercolour. 50 x 25 cm. The Royal Collection © 2012 HM Queen Elizabeth II.

unknown, could have been provoked by the artist's own faith.[69]

The faith of all Britons was put to the test by the apocalypse that was the First World War. When Britain entered the war in August 1914 it was by no means clear what aspects of life would be affected – never mind suspended – by it and, in the event, the patterns of artistic life were variously altered, as James Fox has ably documented.[70] While there was an argument that luxuries such as art should be abandoned – and there were many instance of artists themselves declaring their profession redundant in the face of this cataclysm – there was an equal argument that they were especially cheering as the strife escalated, and in any case there was the question of how artists were to continue to support themselves during the conflict.[71] As the *Burlington Magazine*'s book reviewer wrote, on the re-issue of Fortescue-Brickdale's *Idylls* in a cheaper edition for the 1914 Christmas market, "In the midst of national dangers, domestic sorrows, and financial difficulties ... a good many publishers are exerting themselves to provide pastime and distraction, especially for younger and less critical readers, and they deserve every encouragement for doing so".[72]

Thus, however unintentionally, Fortescue-Brickdale's next 'coloured book' was perhaps helped to a good reception by its underplayed nationalism.[73] The *Book of Old English Songs and Ballads* (p. 74) was published by Hodder and Stoughton in autumn 1915, carrying 24 coloured plates in a belated sequel to the *Idylls* of 1911. It played to the artist's strengths, with the classic Pre-Raphaelite figure in nature visualising 'Barbara Allen', 'The Wish', 'The Bailiff's Daughter of Islington', 'Old Age', 'Who is Silvia?' and other poems. Fortescue-Brickdale's notebooks indicate that in these commissions she wrestled with both the choice of texts for treatment and the ways in which they might be treated, with some designs going through several versions before their definitive form was reached. Her weakness for cherubic cupids (a penchant she shared with Shaw) is in evidence, but the pages were modernised by banishment of the decorative borders which, since the publications of the Kelmscott Press in the 1890s, had been *de rigueur* where Arthurian subject-matter was concerned (see p. 41).

While in 1917, art was included in the National Service Bill's list of non-essential industries which gave a man of the relevant age no protection from conscription, for women artists the question arose, what should they do for or about the war? Fortescue-Brickdale's social circle was inclined to service rather than pacifism and, at the age of 42, she was likely to find two generations of intimates in the line of fire: in the event, although her brother John did serve in France, it seems that no-one close to her was killed.[74] "Women get all the dreariness of war and none of its exhilaration", commented one of the best known female commentators of the war, Vera Brittain, in late 1914; "people say the best thing one can do is to stick consistently to one's ordinary work, but it is easier said than done".[75] The marginality that beset women of the upper classes is glimpsed in a note appearing in the social columns of *The Lady* two years into the war, when the writer is reviewing the opening of the RWS exhibition: "Sir Charles and Lady Fortescue-Brickdale were with Miss Brickdale, who has several of her charming pictures hung. Lady Fortescue-Brickdale is the sister of Lady Hallam Parr and Mrs Cyril Cunard, and is one of the large family of Gloucestershire Gibbs, of which practically every male member is serving with one or other of his Majesty's forces".[76] Some male artists joined the armed services – and Lucy Kemp-Welch was one female artist who tried to – but the most obvious way for artists of either sex to support the war was through fund-raising exhibitions of work – and Fortescue-Brickdale appeared in the RWS exhibition of February 1915 and the vast Red Cross sale in February 1918.[77] She contributed also to the philanthropy expected of her class, serving on the council of the Imperial Arts League (a pre-war organisation designed as a professional body for artists) from April 1914 until the end of 1916, and on the founding committee for the Star and Garter Home in Richmond, for which in 1916 she designed the insignia and a wartime medal for the London ambulance service.[78]

At the end of 1916, the new magazine *Vogue* reflected on Fortescue-Brickdale's showing at the annual RWS exhibition:

> "Before the Old Water-colour Society was half-way through its history, as we have it today, the whole of the art life in England was revolutionised by the Pre-Raphaelite movement. Now only a few little ripples from the wash of that great wave are to be perceived in London picture exhibitions. In this exhibition Miss Fortescue-Brickdale seems to strive to plant us right back into the centre of the movement – seems to make believe that it has not yet spent itself. Her watercolour *Truants* is in this respect a pictorial curiosity, desiring to charm by old association, and perhaps succeeding".[79]

Fortescue-Brickdale's next book project was no unconnected with this spirit. Under the title *Eleanor Fortescue Brickdale's Golden Book of Famous Women* (p. 83), it presented a sisterhood of literary and historical heroines, each portrayed individually alongside the respective text. The authors anchoring it constituted a 'who's who' of English literature in the post-Victorian mind, with no writer more recent than Tennyson, rendering the entire volume somewhat nostalgic. For the third time, an exhibition of the entire sequence of original watercolours promoted the book at The Leicester Galleries of Ernest Brown and Phillips.

Even with a good dealer, as the war dragged on the future of artistic patronage, especially the traditionalist taste on which Fortescue-Brickdale relied, must have seemed precarious, not only because of financial disarray but because of the sea-change in British life generated by the disillusionment of the war years. Dealing with the war experience took various forms, and Fortescue-Brickdale was commissioned to create a kind of testimonial on it [fig. 8] when various women's organisations employed her to create an illuminated address to Queen Mary, to mark the royal couple's silver wedding in mid 1918. "For four anxious years", it read in part, "it has been our dearest wish and earnest endeavour to devote ourselves mind and body to the service of our King and to humbly strive so far as in us lies to assist our Country and our allies in their conflict against our common foe ... It is our dearest hope that before the next anniversary of this day the dark cloud of war may be dispersed." In a further coda to the nightmare, a privately commissioned painting entitled *The Guardian Angel* (1918,

p. 82) was issued as a colour print by the Medici Society in 1921 as a tribute to the wartime service of the RAF.

In 1919, Fortescue-Brickdale's commitment to watercolour was recognised in her belated election to membership of the RWS (p. 77).[80] She continued to send work to the RWS and the RA, as well as to the Liverpool Autumn Exhibition, almost annually until 1927. These works show her to be exploring new stylistic avenues, but how fruitful such practice might be in these changed times was moot: attendance figures at the RA had already been in steady decline before the war, and Virginia Woolf's review of the 1919 exhibition is telling in expressing, not a hostility to its survival, so much as an assumption that its utility by that stage must be as entertainment – not art.[81] There is some evidence that the early 1920s were lean years for artists of all persuasions, as recovery from the war focussed on what were deemed necessities,[82] but for Pre-Raphaelites the end definitely seemed to be in sight: "Through the late Mr Byam Shaw the last phase of pre-Raphaelitism was handed down to Miss EF Brickdale, who may claim to be the last descendant", wrote the *Observer*'s reviewer of her *Golden Book of Famous Women* at the end of 1919; and in the following year a modernist reviewer of the Royal Academy seems only to be expressing the inevitable in his brusque dismissal of Pre-Raphaelitism, grouping Fortescue-Brickdale's work with that of Frank Cadogan Cowper and others as "Wardour Street tableaux-vivants".[83]

In fact, the immediate post-war time was busy for Fortescue-Brickdale. She had resumed some of her previous duties at the Byam Shaw school in the 1918–19 academic year, judging the drapery and antique drawing prizes and taking classes in Composition and Illustration. His unexpected death in 1919 must have added considerably to the strain of these responsibilities, which continued until the end of 1923, when Brickdale herself became severely hampered by illness (of which more in due course). In 1920 she took over Shaw's production of monthly posters for the Maternity and Child Welfare Department's magazine, producing over a dozen black-and-white designs on topics such as breastfeeding and safety at home – perhaps the most contemporary productions in her entire output.

Memorials to individual victims of the war were also in great demand even before it was over, and Fortescue-Brickdale's readiness to design for stained glass led to commissions from the bereaved amongst her patrons, including her most effective sculptural work, a memorial to the war dead of the King's Own Yorkshire Light Infantry, for the regimental chapel in York Minster (*The Angel of Death,* 1919–21, fig. 9). The vocabulary of knights, angels and saints that Fortescue-Brickdale had deployed over the years (see p. 41, and fig. 7) seemed fitting to these clients for mourning and celebrating the rude loss of English servicemen which cast a shadow over Britain at that time. In the 'teams' of sacred figures she devised for her patrons – the three archangels Raphael, Michael and Gabriel who represent Hope, Comfort and Consolation; St George, St Nicholas and St Joan of Arc; Chivalry, Fortitude and Faith – the heroic and the humble were combined to render the 'supreme sacrifice' more bearable.[84] It was a vocabulary potent for these ageing admirers of Tennyson and Arthur, though some later critics deplored it as "an unattractive attempt to spiritualize war and christianize the martial virtues".[85]

A new field of exposure also opened up for the artist in the weekly *Illustrated London News*, which not only publicised her work but gave her several commissions over the next decade. In addition, her 1920 Academy exhibit, *The Forerunner* (p. 86), was bought by Lord Leverhulme, who was amassing one of the biggest private collections of British art, and here it sat among works by many artists working similar territory.[86] In 1922 Fortescue-Brickdale's next illustrated book appeared, *The Sweet and Touching Tale of Fleur and Blanchefleur*, in collaboration with a new publisher, Daniel O'Connor, and in 1925, she

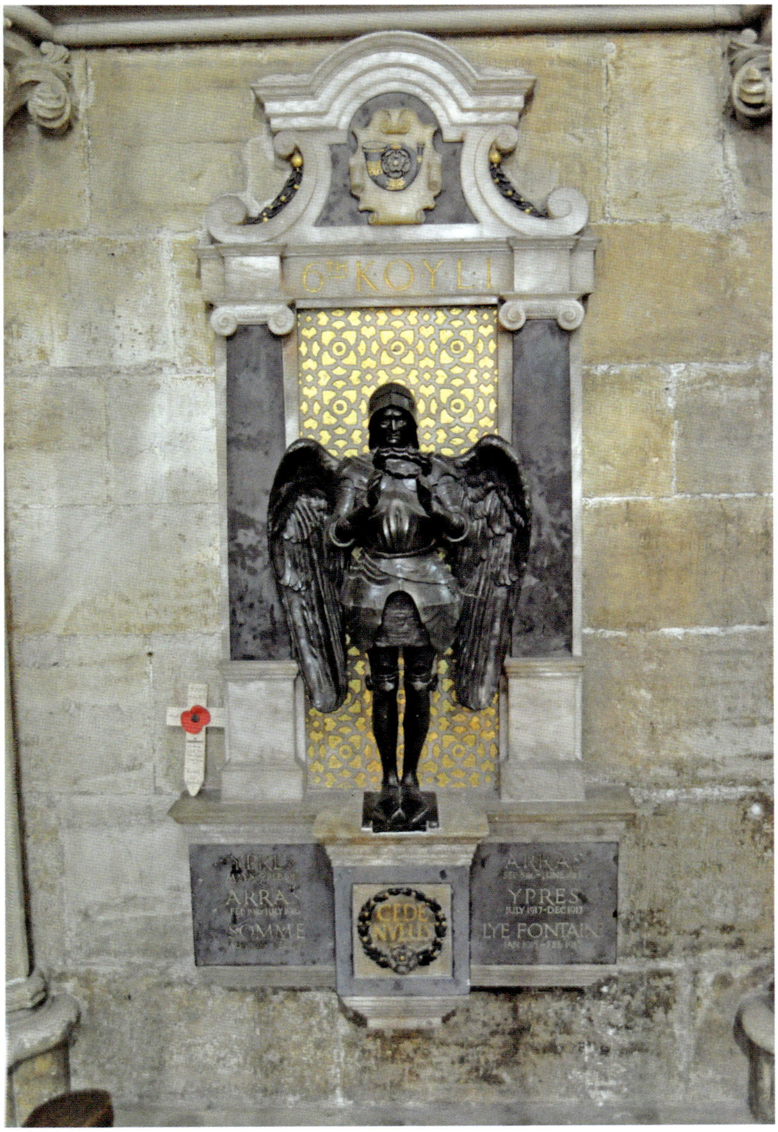

Fig. 9

King's Own Yorkshire Light Infantry (KOYLI) memorial, 1919-21, bronze. H 62 cm. St John's Chapel, York Minster. Reproduced by kind permission of the Dean and Chapter of York

illustrated a book of Christmas carols for the DelaMore Press. While window commissions rapidly succeeded one another, yet another kind of work - altarpieces - expanded her repertoire.

It is perhaps hardly surprising that the 50 year-old artist fell seriously ill in the early 1920s. In June 1923 a friend's diary records, "Bricky is better but her hands are still bandaged", while in the September Byam Shaw's son George wrote to a mutual friend, "Isn't it dreadful about the bad time poor Eleanor has been having? She is so good and patient but she has masses of work to do and can't touch a pencil". In the December the commissioners of an altarpiece for St Barnabas church in Sutton, south London (known as *Christ in Majesty*, fig. 10), heard from Charles Fortescue-Brickdale that "his sister is slowly recovering from her long illness and hopes to resume work in January".[87] As it was, she spent the last part of 1923 convalescing at Amélie les Bains, the Pyrenean spa town.

As a consequence of this illness (as yet unidentified), Fortescue-Brickdale's sight began to deteriorate, leading her to favour larger-scale work rather than the finely worked watercolours in which she had specialised. The St Barnabas altarpiece was followed by one for the Chapel of Remembrance in the British Empire Exhibition at Wembley in 1924. Christopher Whall, Phoebe Stabler, JE Nuttgens and F Derwent Wood were amongst the artists contributing to the other five chapels.[88] Like the *Christ in Majesty*, this was a tripartite composition with a central standing figure, presumably St Michael (a heavenly surrogate for St George), flanked by groups of figures worshipping, hailing or otherwise paying him respect. The Empire altarpiece appears distinctly masculine compared with *Christ in Majesty*: there, Christ was honoured by feminine angels, draped and winged, and robed clergy, against a rich night sky and standing on a carpet of anemones, whereas at the British Empire exhibition a starker, almost stentorian, martial tone is struck, as the various male figures gesture fervently against a low horizon on which a distant city lurks.

Both these works functioned as war memorials, which was less obviously the case with the third altarpiece that Fortescue-Brickdale accomplished in this period. The triptych *Knightly Service* was commissioned in 1924 by Montague Rendall, the former headmaster of Winchester College for boys, Hampshire, who described it as "representing the spirit of a Public School, especially in Wartime".[89] Though her nephews Matthew and Edmund were pupils of the College, it was not the family connection but her patron's belief that they shared a sensibility that brought Fortescue-

Brickdale the commission. A patron of the artist's since 1906, he also bought the painting *Botticelli's Studio*, her 1922 sequel to *The Forerunner* (1920, p. 86), two compositions celebrating the artist as a lynchpin of civilised society.[90] Various trips to continental Europe over the years had taken Fortescue-Brickdale to Italy and, though Leonardo da Vinci and Sandro Botticelli were not necessarily her specific favourites – echoes of Perugino and other literally Pre-Raphaelite painters sound more loudly in her work – she and Rendall shared a love for early Italian art. The College triptych, summed up by a friend of the artist's as covering "all the phases of a boy's school life, including a rugger scrum",[91] sprang from Rendall's notion that "the public school system derives from schools of chivalry in medieval castles, masters, prefects, and lower boys corresponding to knights, squires, and pages".[92] The largest of Fortescue-Brickdale's works, its curious 'stylelessness' may be due to the artist's contemporary doubts about the continuing validity of Pre-Raphaelitism.

Fortescue-Brickdale's last solo 'coloured book' appeared in 1925. This was *Palgrave's Golden Treasury of Songs and Lyrics* for Hodder and Stoughton (p. 90). First published in 1861 and much reissued, it reflected the taste of its time – though Palgrave had invited future generations to adapt his selection. This edition bore twelve coloured plates by the artist, whose choice of texts allowed her to shift her attention from the medieval, which had so occupied her over the years, to the Jacobean and Carolingian – as in the illustration to Robert Herrick, *'Whenas in silks my Julia goes'* – still nevertheless a quintessentially Pre-Raphaelite drawing, as its preparatory study shows. With 288 verses in the book, twelve illustrations hardly scratched the surface of its pictorial potential, and this modest amount of pictorial content probably reflects Fortescue-Brickdale's limited capacity to work on fine detail since her illness. Even though this was her last publication of this kind – which sophisticates had found already stale at the start of the decade[93] – she did later book work, for her friend Dion Clayton Calthrop's *Diary of an eighteenth-century Garden* (1926) and *The Gentle Art* (1927).

Though the late 1920s brought a marked decrease in Fortescue-Brickdale's exhibition appearances, these years saw a number of her window designs realised in churches large and small around the country, echoing the Burne-Jones legacy of stained glass work for Morris and Company which brought Pre-Raphaelitism into so many English communities. These included the sad mission of commemorating the younger of her two brothers, John, who had died in 1921. The window sacred to him and two other members of the congregation of his church, All Saints' Clifton (Bristol), installed in 1928, reiterated the family's long connection not only with that city but with the south-western region that covers Avon, south Gloucestershire, and northern Somerset. This area today sees a larger concentration of Fortescue-Brickdale's work than any other, consolidated in her last active decade by window designs in the city's Anglican Cathedral (1927), St Andrew's in Chew Magna (1934, p. 95) and St Audries in West Quantoxhead (1939), and her last altarpiece (about 1933) in All Saints' church, Newland, the Wye valley village home of her grandparents and aunt and the setting of various compositions over the years (p. 73). In these commissions her long-established repertoire of knights, saints and angels was appropriate, amplified with narrative vignettes, whether the venue was a church, chapel or benevolent institution.

Though Fortescue-Brickdale remained creatively active well into her sixties, the sense of decline if not closure expressed in her already cited complaint of 1927 that "Pre-Raphaelitism is no longer wanted", is echoed in a large painting she embarked upon in 1929 in which she assembled colleagues, friends and relatives in the benign presence of Mary the mother of Jesus. In valedictory manner, they each embody a different century ('from the 1st century up to the present day'), which is represented by the banner each holds up

Fig. 10
Christ in Majesty,
St Barnabas, Sutton,
1923–24, oil.
48 x 180 cm.

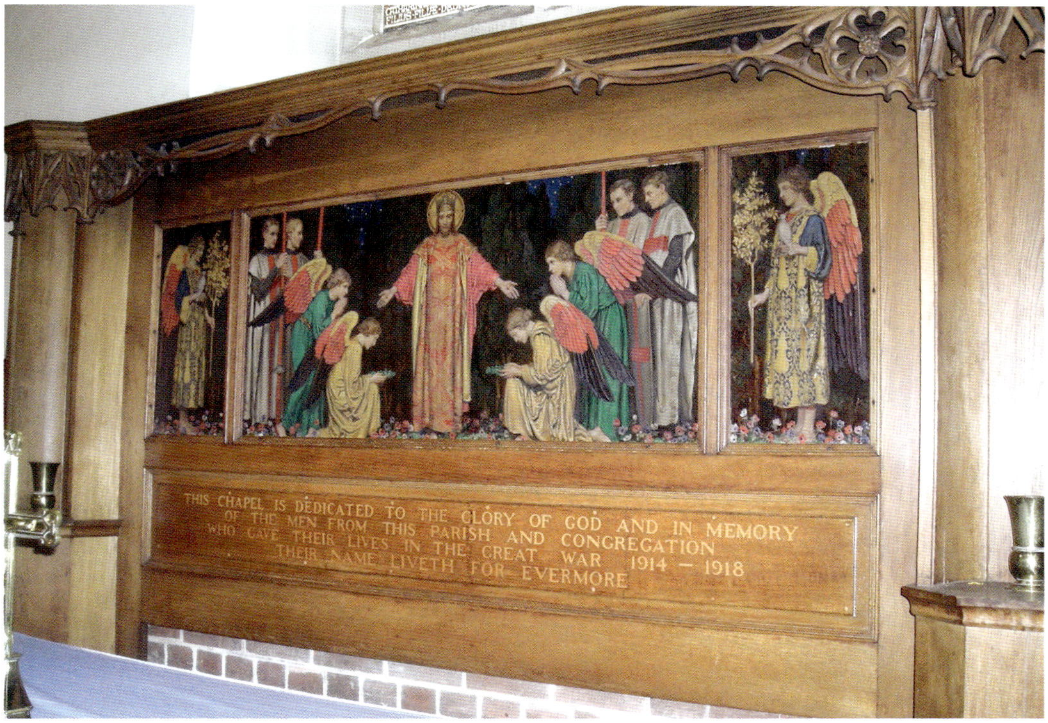

and made clear by their period costume – the latter always a staple feature of Fortescue-Brickdale's repertoire. Letters to her brother Charles – who figured in the composition – show that it was a self-imposed task, for which the artist did not expect to find a buyer.[94]

Major works after this date – *Prospero and Ariel* painted for the new Broadcasting House in London (1931–2), an Elgar memorial window (1934–5), a church window for the Barnardo's Barkingside home for girls – have either been lost (the first) or did not eventuate (the latter two), and a stroke in 1938 meant that Fortescue-Brickdale's was one of many careers that did not survive the outbreak of the Second World War in the following year. When her obituary identified Fortescue-Brickdale as "the last survivor of the later Pre-Raphaelite painters", it claimed that "she deserves to be remembered for her consistent fidelity to that tradition".[95] This was at a point when Pre-Raphaelitism finally seemed to be an art of the past, and modernity had won the day. As a rule, women artists are hard to place in the dominant 'isms' that Art History has established, but it was certainly Fortescue-Brickdale's achievement to sustain that particular style and its meanings as the Victorian period gave way to the modern era. But in addition, her career also demonstrates now, from the vantage point of the early 21st century, both the difficulties of the journey that had to be made by Brickdale's generation and the durability of 19th-century tastes. From the Victorian age to the modern day lay a winding route, and Eleanor Fortescue-Brickdale's life's work is a testament to its complexity.

Notes

1 Cecily Peele diaries, vol. 1, 16 April 1927, Shropshire Archives. My thanks go to Nancy Anderson and John Peele for facilitating my access to this material.
2 Arundel Society, established in 1849 to preserve and record works of art vulnerable to destruction; Ruskin was on its council from the start.
3 See Charles' letter to *The Times,* 9 March 1932, p. 8.
4 Norwood Society, *Conservation in Norwood,* 1986, p. 7.
5 Respectively, Austin Fryer, *Historical Souvenir of the Crystal Palace,* Daily Express Publications, 1901, p. 113, and Anonymous, *Crystal Palace: the official guide to the Palace and Park,* RK Burt and co, undated, p. 55.
6 Fortescue-Brickdale quoted in James Cassidy, "The Palace Beautiful", *The Ludgate,* September 1898, p. 425.
7 See Tessa Mackenzie, *The Art Schools of London,* Chapman and Hall, 1895, pp. 30-1.
8 See "Notes on Current Events", *The British Architect,* 31 July 1891, p. 80 and "International Horticultural Exhibition", *The Times,* 2 August 1892, p. 2.
9 Mackenzie, p. 70.
10 St John's Wood 1896, RA Schools 1897-1902.
11 "Behind much - some would say, behind all - of the best Edwardian art there lay that great forcing-house, the Slade School" (John Russell, 'Art', *Edwardian England 1901-1914,* London: Oxford University Press, 1964, p. 340).
12 Marion Hepworth Dixon, "Our rising Artists: Eleanor Fortescue-Brickdale", *The Magazine of Art,* 25, 1902, p. 257.
13 Another tailpiece by the artist ("The Undecided Man", p. 27) and a new headpiece ("Conrad Reuter of Second Avenue", p. 80) appeared in the same journal in January 1896.
14 Eleanor Fortescue-Brickdale, "The Artist's Career as a practical Profession for Women", *Women's Employment,* 15 January 1932, p. 28.
15 *Design for an advertisement,* No. 1494.
16 See typically "Royal Academy Students Competitions", *The British Architect,* 17 December 1897, p. 454. The winning design appeared at the next RA exhibition (1898) as *Spring,* no. 1198.
17 She was credited in the closing words of the author's preface as Miss EF Brickdale (Gibbs, *A Cotswold Village or County Life and Pursuits in Gloucestershire,* John Murray, 1898, p. viii; photographs by Colonel Mordaunt also helped to illustrate the book. By 1918, it was in its third edition).
18 "To many young men [sic] beside myself he gave a start in life by obtaining commissions for them and introducing them to collectors of works of art" (Frank Cadogan Cowper, Brickdale's contemporary at the RA and Abbey's assistant, quoted in EV Lucas, *Edwin Austin Abbey,* Methuen/Scribner, 1921. p. 372). Fortescue-Brickdale (and Shaw) assisted Cowper on 1902 commissions connected with Edward VII's coronation (FCC to his mother, COW/1/5, Royal Academy Archives). Abbey himself was inclined to borrow from other artists - a practice it can be supposed he recommended to his students (see *Edwin Austin Abbey,* Yale University Art Gallery, 1973).
19 Roger Fry, Duncan Grant, Vanessa Bell and their friends, commonly known now as the Bloomsbury Group, were seen to be behind the rise of avant-garde art: see Richard Shone, *The Art of Bloomsbury,* Tate Gallery Publishing, 1999.
20 Roy Strong, *Country Life 1897-1997. The English Arcadia,* Country Life Books, 1996, p. 29. For an appraisal of *The Ladies' Field,* see Kate Jackson, *George Newnes and the New Journalism in Britain 1880-1910,* Ashgate, 2001, pp. 209-35.
21 This opportunity was credited by Hepworth Dixon (p. 257) to a personal introduction to Newnes.
22 Fortescue-Brickdale's importance in forming the magazine's image is indicated in Strong's book: its endpapers carry a sampler of head and tailpieces from the first decade of publication: of the 20 designs used, ten are by Brickdale, though the text fails to credit any of the illustrators except Byam Shaw. Her connection with *The Ladies' Field* seems to have lasted only a year.
23 Thus for instance, as well as Condover, Coggeshall, the medieval village where the Noel Buxtons' historic home Paycockes was situated; and Biddesden, the country seat of the Gribble and then the Baring families.
24 "And book-plates! all the newest crazes, you see..." ("Mrs Percy Dearmer at Home", *The Sketch,* 26 June 1895, p. 485). See "Modern Book-plates and their Designers", *Studio,* 15:67, October 1898, p. 43.

25 Gerald Taylor, *Centenary Exhibition of Works by Eleanor Fortescue Brickdale*, Ashmolean Museum, 1972–3, p. 3. In the next census (1901), she identified herself as 'artist sculptor on own account'.

26 What Pre-Raphaelitism might be at the turn of the century had been canvassed in mid 1898 by the influential magazine *The Studio* in its regular opinion-piece: "The Lay Figure and Pre-Raphaelitism", *The Studio*, 13:59, February 1898, p. 70. Of later attempts to sum up Pre-Raphaelitism, one of the best is Inga Bryden's introduction to Bryden ed., *The Pre-Raphaelites: writings and sources* (4 vols), Routledge/Thoemmes, London, 1998 (pp. 1–31).

27 EBS, "Eleanor F. Brickdale, designer and illustrator", *The Studio*, 13:60, March 1898, pp. 103–8; it has been speculated, though no evidence has ever been adduced, that the author was Evelyn Pyke-Knott, by then Evelyn Byam Shaw. A few months later, she was presented in *The Ladies' Field* as a black-and-white artist (EME, "Miss Eleanor Fortescue Brickdale: artist in black-and-white", *The Ladies' Field*, 2:24, 27 August 1898, pp. 502–3). Simon Houfe puts her at this point in the company of Laurence Housman, Paul Woodroffe, Herbert Cole, and Byam Shaw (Simon Houfe, *Fin-de-siecle: illustrators of the Nineties*, Barrie and Jenkins, 1992, pp. 32–6).

28 See the present author's "Time and Tide wait for no man: a Victorian apocalypse", Christian Heck and Kristen Lippincott eds., *Symbols of Time in the History of Art*, Brepols, 2002, pp. 85-97.

29 See Caroline Dakers, *The Holland Park Circle*, Yale University Press, 1999, though she has little to say about Fortescue-Brickdale (p. 221). Brickdale left the RA Schools at the end of 1899.

30 Though the following year, when many were re-exhibited, the catalogue showed that several had been bought by the Dowdeswells themselves.

31 Tellingly, Hughes worked as an illustrator until 1904, while Hunt was a focus of interest up until 1907, through his reminiscences of the movement and the debate about the public acquisition of his late version of *The Lady of Shalott*; see Susan Casteras ed., *Pocket Cathedrals: pre-Raphaelite book illustration*, Yale Center for British Art, 1991 and Judith Bronkhurst, *William Holman Hunt, a catalogue raisonné*, Yale University Press, 2006.

32 See, for example, Wyke Bayliss, *Five Great Painters of the Victorian Era*, London, 1902, which celebrated Leighton, Millais, Burne-Jones, Holman Hunt and Watts; and, latterly, the exhibitions The Last Romantics (Barbican Art Gallery, London, 1989) and Heaven on Earth (Djanogly Art Gallery, Nottingham, 1994); see their catalogues, John Christian ed., *The Last Romantics: the romantic tradition in British art*, Lund Humphries, 1989 (reprinted 1993, 1995, 1998) and Gail-Nina Anderson and Joanne Wright, *Heaven on Earth: the religion of beauty in late Victorian art*, Djanogly Art Gallery, 1994.

33 "Miss Brickdale", *The Artist*, 31, June 1901, pp. 205–6.

34 Published by Hodder and Stoughton, who were later responsible for some of the artist's most important commissions. Sparrow grouped her with Marianne Stokes and Mary Young Hunter (p. 71). For a critique of his approach that is still favourable to Brickdale, see GRH, "A later Pre-Raphaelite", *Pall Mall Gazette*, 21 June 1901, p. 1.

35 A critical tendency to identify Fortescue-Brickdale as Shaw's imitator or follower had already begun (see MH Spielmann, "Royal Academy II", *The Magazine of Art*, 22, June 1899, p. 387; Anon, "Art Centres", *The Artist*, May 1901, p. 98; and see "Mr Byam Shaw's Pictures", *The Times*, 12 June 1902, p. 14 for a repudiation of the idea that *he* was influenced by *her*). This stemmed from the widespread reflex that assumed women's lack of originality and men's authority. The artist's own opinion of her subordination is not recorded, but she remained close to Shaw and his family until the end of her life. It is assumed they met at the RA Schools, since he left St John's Wood before she enrolled there (though Charles Fortescue-Brickdale and Shaw had both attended Westminster School); she was god-mother to his daughter Barbara, from 1904–6 she lived with his mother, was bridesmaid at his sister Margaret's wedding in 1913, and four members of the Shaw family were beneficiaries of Brickdale's will in 1945.

36 Fortescue-Brickdale's name makes no appearance in the records of suffragist circles, though neither does it in the ranks of the anti-suffragists. On suffrage art and artists, see Lisa Tickner, *The Spectacle of*

Women, Chatto and Windus, 1987. Later on, liberal feminists such as Frances Balfour and the Picton-Turbeville sisters were amongst Brickdale's patrons.

37 Ruskin to William E Wilcox (undated), quoted by Judith Bronkhurst, "Words and Images: the Pre-Raphaelites and Literature" in Mikael Ahlund ed., *The Pre-Raphaelites*, Nationalmuseum Stockholm, 2009, p. 113; Ruskin expressed a similar view to Tennyson himself, saying "it does not so much matter whether any given vignette is right or not, as whether it contains thought or not" (Ruskin to Tennyson [24 July 1857], quoted by Julia Thomas in Jim Cheshire ed., *Tennyson Transformed: Alfred Lord Tennyson and Victorian visual culture*, Lund Humphries, 2009, p. 30).

38 His biographer Emilie Russell Barrington reported: "In 1902, when speaking to me in terms of unbounded admiration of Miss Fortescue-Brickdale's work, he said to me, 'I feel inclined to throw away my palette and brushes. What are my things by the side of such stuff as hers'". (Mrs Russell Barrington, *GF Watts: Reminiscences*, George Allen, 1905, p. 199.) For Watts' significance at this point in time, see Laurence Binyon, "Watts and National Art", *Independent Review*, 5:18, February–April 1905, pp. 201–9.

39 *Miss Eleanor Fortescue-Brickdale*, no 109 (private collection). Brickdale herself joined the Pastel Society in 1904, but exhibited with it that year only, although she remained a member until 1909.

40 Sichel to MW Cornish, July 1901 in Edith Sichel, *Letters, Verses and other Writings*, Emily M Ritchie ed., privately published 1918, p. 110. Sichel's article was "A Woman-Painter and Symbolism", *Monthly Review*, 4:12, September 1901, pp. 101–114.

41 Hodgkins to Isabel Field, March 1902 in Linda Gill ed., *Letters of Frances Hodgkins*, Auckland University Press, 1993, p. 121. Fortescue-Brickdale's repute in the colonies, also attested to by Thea Proctor, one of Australia's most influential 20th-century artists, was achieved largely through the illustrated press which played a great part in forming artistic opinion in those parts (see Proctor to Mrs Irvine, 20 November 1903 quoted by Helen Morgan, "Thea Proctor the Artist: Career before 1921 and the Question of Aesthetic Reputation". Master's thesis, University of Melbourne, 1994, p. 31).

42 "Art and Artists", *Otago Witness*, 11 June 1902, p. 70.

43 "The Royal Academy. Second notice", *The Athenaeum*, 16 May 1903, p. 632; Charles Holme ed., *Representative Art of our Time*, published in five parts, 1903 (see *Youth and the Lady*, part V).

44 "The Society of Oil Painters", *The Times*, 9 January 1902, p. 6; this verdict is seen across the range of the British press: see "Art Notes", *The Illustrated London News*, 6 December 1902, p. 876 and "Art", *The Academy and Literature*, 6 December 1902, p. 635.

45 Walter Shaw Sparrow, "The Glasgow International Exhibition", *The Studio*, 23:99, June 1901, p. 44.

46 In reviewing the show, *The Times* commented on the artist's emulation of Watts' example ("Art Exhibitions", 13 June 1905, p. 12), and, squaring the circle, some commentators linked him explicitly with Pre-Raphaelitism (see "Mr Watts' Pictures", *The Athenaeum*, 4 April 1903, p. 440). Watts and Brickdale were near neighbours in Holland Park at this time.

47 See *Love and Adversity* (1900), *St Michael with a Captive Woman* (1904).

48 Alfred Lord Tennyson, *Poems*, Bell and Hyman, 1905. This was in the Endymion series, which had already seen Robert Anning Bell illustrate Keats and Shelley, Byam Shaw Browning and W Heath Robinson Poe (see Gordon Ray, *The Illustrator and the Book in England from 1790 to 1914*, Pierpont Morgan Library/ Oxford University Press, 1976, pp. 182–4).

49 Stopford A Brooke, *Tennyson: his art and relation to modern life*, Isbister and co, London, 1894 (reprinted 1894, 1894, 1898; second edition 1900); for the continued appearance of Arthurian subject-matter on the London stage, see Beverley Taylor and Elisabeth Brewer, *The Return of King Arthur*, DS Brewer, 1983, ch. 7.

50 George S Layard, *Tennyson and his Pre-Raphaelite Illustrators*, E Stock, 1894; various anniversary and commemorative London exhibitions had reminded the gallery-going public of them, e.g. Burne-Jones at the New Gallery 1892–3 and 1898–9, Millais at the RA 1898. A reminder in book form from the very same George Bell and Sons was Percy Bate's history of Pre-Raphaelitism, *The English Pre-Raphaelite Painters, their Associates and Successors* (1899), reissued in a revised version in 1901, and reprinted in 1902, 1905 and 1910.

51 CL Hind, "Ethical Art and Mr F Cayley Robinson", *The Studio*, 31:133, April 1904,

pp. 238-9. Fortescue-Brickdale was again linked with Cayley Robinson (and Abbey, Shaw and Frank Craig) in "a small band of painters" animated by "a distinctive principle of truthful endeavour" in R Trafford, "The Art of Mr Frank Craig', *Windsor Magazine*, 28:3, August 1908, pp. 247-63.

52 The work for Liberty was reported in *The Studio*, "Studio-talk", 32:138, September 1904, pp. 344-5; as Liberty's did not record the names of designers/artists who worked for them, it is difficult to know if this connection grew or endured: see *Liberty's 1875-1975*, Victoria and Albert Museum, 1975, pp. 13-16, 53-64.

53 Anonymous, "Famous Women Workers", *The Queen*, 30 July 1904, p. 195; later Brickdale sculptures were all statuettes: *Angel of Death* (1918-21), *St Thomas More* and *St John Fisher* (1937), *Virgin and Child* (1938). A 1918 studio photo of Brickdale shows a statuette of the Virgin and Child in progress which may be a further work. Significantly, in *The Year's Art* for 1904, Brickdale has herself listed as an art worker/craftswoman rather than simply a painter (ACR Carter ed., *The Year's Art*, Hutchinson and Co, 1904, p. 407).

54 See Susan Beattie, *The New Sculpture*, Yale University Press, 1983 and, for specific instances of shared sympathies, Alfred Gilbert's Clarence Tomb figures, 1892-9; George Frampton, *Guinevere*, Astor House, 1895-6; Robert Anning Bell, *Music* and *Dancing*, 1897; William Reynolds-Stephens, *Chivalry*, RA 1910; and various works by William Reynolds-Stephens.

55 Mabel Dearmer, *A Child's Life of Christ*, Methuen, 1906.

56 Some of these are compared in Debra Mancoff, *The Return of King Arthur*, Harry N Abrams, 1995 and Barbara Tepa and Alan Lupack, *Illustrating Camelot*, DS Brewer, 2008. For Forbes, see Cook, Hardie and Payne, *Singing from the Walls: the life and art of Elizabeth Forbes*, Sansom and Company, 2000.

57 See, for instance, "Art Books", *Burlington Magazine*, 14:70, January 1909, p. 248; "Reviews", *The New Age*, 4 February 1909, p. 306; "Other Exhibitions", *The Athenaeum*, 24 July 1909, p. 104; "Art Books", *Burlington Magazine*, 16:81, December 1909, p. 169.

58 Anonymous, *"Three Summer Pageants"*, *Review of Reviews*, June 1907, pp. 589-90. On this craze, see Deborah Sugg Ryan, "Spectacle, the Public and the Crowd" in O'Neill and Hatt eds., *The Edwardian Sense*, Yale University Press, 2010.

59 Anonymous, "Reviews: Gift Books", *Burlington Magazine*, 18:93, December 1910, p. 193.

60 The first volume was published in book form in May, the second in October. Other contributors were Beatrice Parsons, Anna Lea Merritt, Hugh Norris, Lilian Stannard, Margaret Waterfield, A Fairfax Muckley, Francis James, Harold Ackerman and Marie Low.

61 For example, "Studio-Talk", *The Studio*, 54:224, October 1911, pp. 143-4.

62 Valentine Cunningham ed., *The Victorians*, Blackwell, 2000, p. 333. The choice for the publicity puff of "Eleanor F Brickdale's delicate and dainty illustrations reveal a vivid fancy no less than technical skill" from the *Glasgow Herald* shows the publisher's strategy of capitalising on this possible defect (advertisement, *The Athenaeum*, 29 January 1909, p. 113).

63 For the meaning of the Arthurian stories, see Taylor and Brewer, Introduction, and Christine Poulson, *The Quest for the Grail: Arthurian Legend in British Art 1840-1920*, Manchester University Press, 1999: on the Idylls, ch. 2 and on its treatment of women and men, ch. 9.

64 *Tennyson's Guinevere and other Poems*, illustrated by Florence Harrison, Blackie and Son, 1912. Some Arthurian subject-matter was contained also in her edition of William Morris, *Early Poems*, Blackie and Son, 1914. The comparable work of their colleague Jessie King is often described as feminine, though it manifests an independence foreign to femininity (see William Morris, *The Defence of Guinevere and other Poems*, John Lane/Bodley Head, 1904).

65 Information from King's College for Women's Council minute books. On Shaw's school, see Timothy Barringer, *Before and after Modernism: Byam Shaw, Rex Vicat Cole, Yinka Shonibare MBE*, Central Saint Martins College of Art and Design, 2010, ch. 7.

66 Other members of staff advertised in 1910 were Byam Shaw's wife, the former Evelyn Pyke-Knott, Carton Moore-Park, D Murray Smith, W Dacres Adams, T Peyton Beale, Percival Silley and C Austin Cooper (e.g. *Art Chronicle*, 11 June 1910, no pagination; *Burlington Magazine*, 17:89, August 1910,

p. vi). The Visitors (external experts) were Murray, Henry Tuke and Charles Sims. In 1911, *The Studio* noted Sims, Shaw, Cole, Brickdale, and Dacres Adams ("Art School Notes", *The Studio*, 51:214, January 1911, p. 336). The artists involved all had personal ties to Shaw. Amongst the 19 patrons recruited to bolster the School's image, drawn from a wider pool, there were no female artists. The most detailed account of the School after Cole's biography (Rex Vicat Cole, *The Art and Life of Byam Shaw*, Seeley Service and co., 1932) is Barringer's.

67 Cole's later biography of Shaw (see above), Valentine Waterhouse's group portrait commemorating the school's opening, and Gladys Beattie Crozier, "Where to Study", *Everywoman's Encyclopaedia*, 1910–11, p. 1159, an article recommending the school to female students.

68 A touching sign of the firm's long relationship with the artist is Harry Grylls' attendance at her funeral on 17 March 1945.

69 For example, *An Opportunity* (1901), *The Greatest of these is Charity* (1905), *The Legend of St Giles* (about 1910), *St Christopher* (1913), *The Good Shepherd* (1916), *I am the true Vine* (1918).

70 James Fox, "Fiddling while Rome is burning: hostility to art during the First World War 1914–18", *Visual Culture in Britain*, 11:1, March 2010, pp. 49–66; he identifies by 1917 the specific claim that both the making of art and its acquisition – thus, both artists and patrons – are unpatriotic. See "The Lay Figure on Art and War", *The Studio*, 63:259, October 1914, for some contemporary thoughts on the general question.

71 Fox cites extreme examples of the anti-art argument from 1915 and 1917, note 50, p. 63. It is curious that Fortescue-Brickdale had no work in the 1916 Women's Exhibition held at the London premises of Waring and Gillow, with the aim of creating "a fund to assist women artists who are sufferers by the War" ("Exhibition of Works of Art by Women Artists", *Colour*, June 1915, p. 157; exhibitors included Brickdale's contemporaries Laura Knight, Flora Lion and Hilda Fearon).

72 Anonymous, "Reviews", *Burlington Magazine*, 26:141, December 1914, p. 132.

73 "Invited to see 'War Exhibitions' at The Leicester Galleries, we find one of the shows there (Miss Brickdale's drawings) has really no bearing at all on the war, except perhaps that it appeals to those of the public who seek in art a refuge from the all-pervading obsession" ("War Exhibitions and War Cartoons", *The Athenaeum*, 9 October 1915, p. 249). *The Studio* reviewer hazarded that the work's Englishness made it appropriate viewing for the time ("Studio-talk", *The Studio*, 66:272, November 1915, p. 136).

74 Though this compromised John's health for the rest of his life; their great-nephew Anthony was killed in the Second World War, serving in Madagascar with the Royal Fusiliers.

75 Brittain to Roland Leighton 1 October 1914, in Bishop and Bostridge eds, *Letters from a Lost Generation*, Northeastern University Press, 1998, p. 31. Some six months later (April 1915), the government called for all able-bodied women to register for both skilled and unskilled work to replace men who had gone into active service. In July 1915, erstwhile suffragists mustered by Emmeline Pankhurst marched for 'women's right to serve' (see Diana Condell and Jean Liddiard, *Working for Victory?*, Routledge and Kegan Paul, London, 1987).

76 Anonymous, "The Lady in Society", *The Lady*, 2 November 1916, p. 512.

77 February 2 1915: no. 121 *The Aeroplane*; April 8/15/22 1918: No. 1822 *Guinevere III: Before the coming of the sinful Queen* (presented by Ernest Brown and Phillips).

78 Described by Estella Canziani, *Round about Three Palace Green*, Methuen, 1939, p. 297.

79 "Exhibition of the Royal Society of Painters in Watercolour", *Vogue*, 1 December 1916, pp. 56–7 (ill. p. 57).

80 Fortescue-Brickdale did not gain membership of the RA, but then it did not elect any woman until 1923 (Annie Swynnerton, elected to associateship too late according to Academy rules to be elevated to full membership). Laura Knight was the eventual ground-breaker (associate 1927, full member 1936).

81 See Mary Anne Stevens in *The Edwardians and After: the Royal Academy 1900–1950*, Royal Academy of Arts/Weidenfeld and Nicolson, 1988, p. 17 and Virginia Woolf, "The Royal Academy", *The Athenaeum*, 22 August 1919.

82 See, for instance, "How some men and women artists are successfully adapting themselves to prevailing conditions", *The Studio*, 83:350, May 1922, p. ix.

83 Respectively, "Miss E.F. Brickdale", *The*

Observer, 28 December 1919, p. 4 and Roy Wilenski, "Fine Arts", *The Athenaeum*, 7 May 1920, p. 611.

84 Respectively, for St Mary's Olveston (1918), Great Welnetham Church, Bury St Edmunds (1918) and St Mary's Church, Taunton (1920).

85 Aylmer and Cant eds., *A History of York Minster*, Clarendon Press, 1977, p. 483; the authors cite Brickdale's memorial as an exemplification of this regrettable tendency.

86 See Edward Morris, *Victorian and Edwardian Paintings in the Lady Lever Art Gallery*, HMSO, 1994, pp. 37-8.

87 Respectively, Molly Sutton diary 6 June 1923, 6710/1, Shropshire Archives; George Byam Shaw to Molly Sutton, 19 September 1923, private collection, New Zealand; and *St Barnabas Church, Sutton, Parish Magazine*, December 1923, p. 2. My thanks go to Nancy Anderson and Humphrey Clarke, respectively, for their kind assistance with these sources.

88 The basilica and its constituent elements are illustrated in Anonymous, *Illustrated Souvenir of the Palace of Arts, British Empire Exhibition*, Fleetway Press, 1924, pp. 129-35.

89 Winchester College Archive, P4/64. My thanks go to Suzanne Foster, the College archivist, for her kind assistance with this material.

90 *The Forerunner* had a spiritual as much as an aesthetic agenda, referring to the last novel of the Russian writer Merezhkovsky's *Christ and Anti-Christ* trilogy (published 1896-1905, trans. 1912), of great interest to idealists just before the war (see Vera Brittan's comments, in Bishop and Bostridge eds., p. 17). In the novel, Leonardo's significance is derived almost more from his rationalist, humanist stance than from his artistic talents.

91 Cecily Peele diaries, vol. 1, 16 April 1927, Shropshire Archives.

92 JD'E Firth, *Rendall of Winchester*, 1954, p. 226n.

93 "Reviews: ornamental books", *Burlington Magazine*, 36:202, January 1920, p. 45. See Michael Felmingham, *The Illustrated Gift Book 1880-1930*, Scolar Press, 1988: "Together with a Lutyens house, a Jekyll garden or a Daimler car, they were tokens of Edwardian refinement" (p. 5).

94 It found a home as an altarpiece for the Kensington church of St George's, Campden Hill. I am grateful to Dave Walker, of the Local Studies section of the Kensington Central Library, for making available to me unpublished documents regarding this work.

95 "Miss Fortescue Brickdale", *The Times*, 14 March 1945, p. 7.

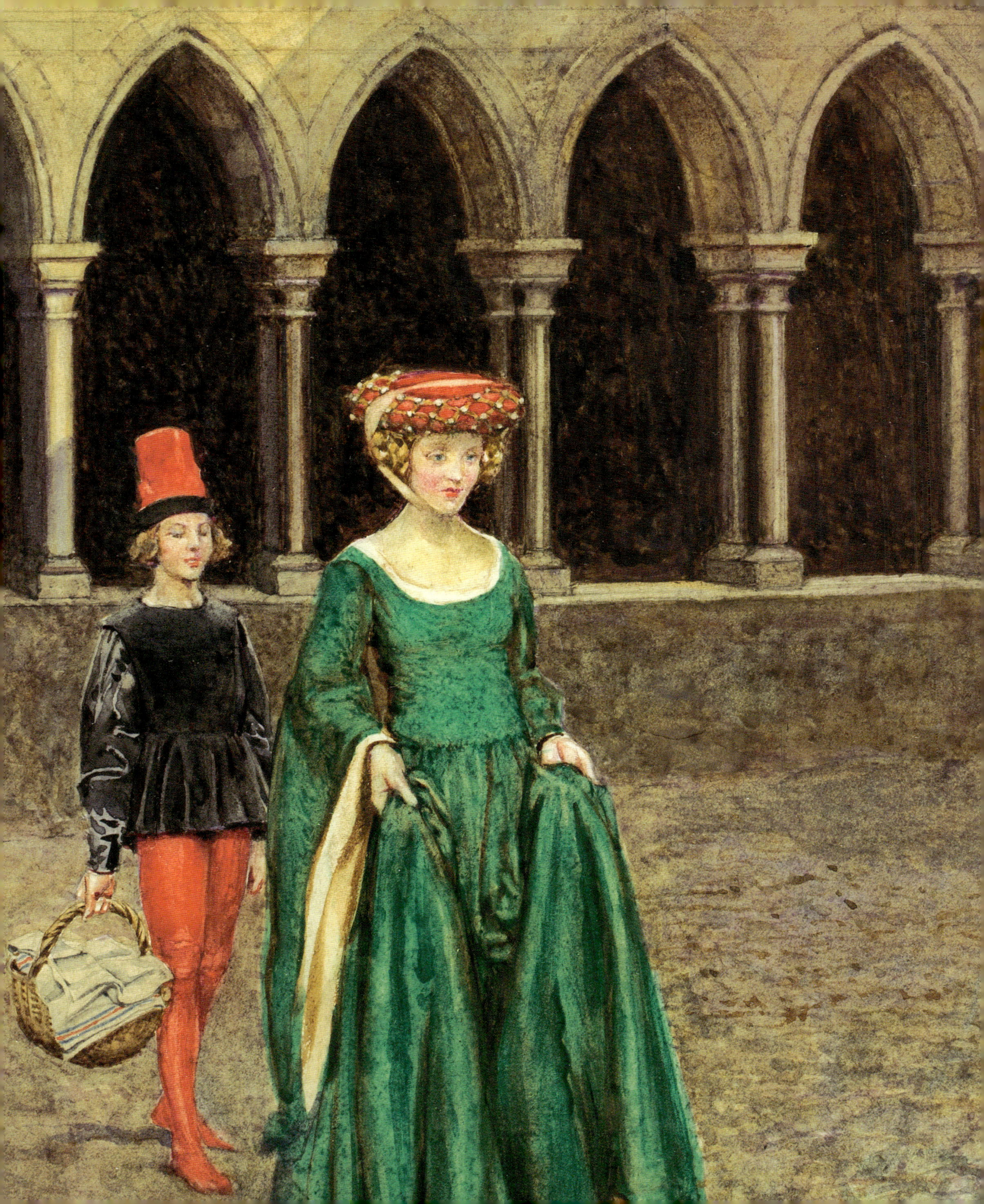

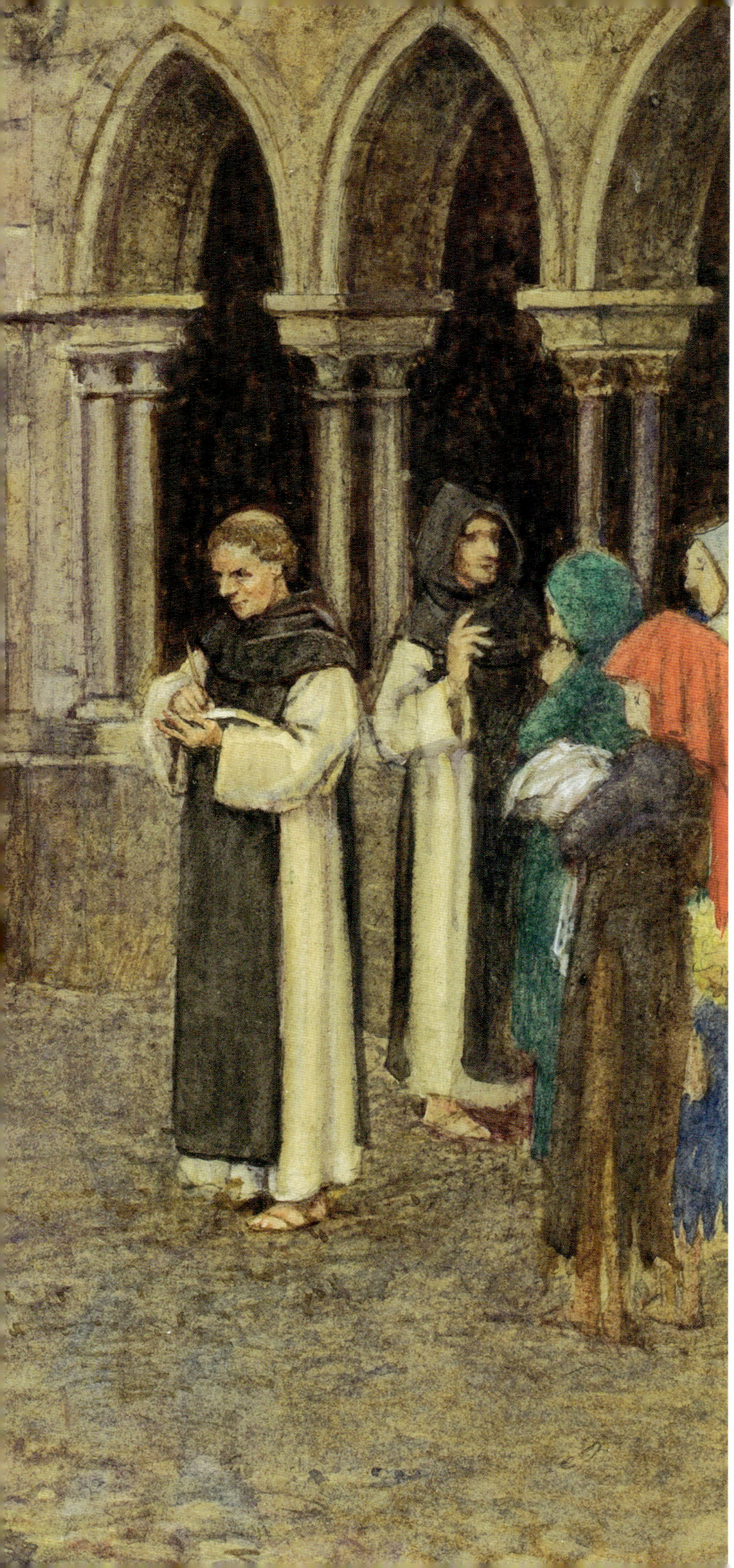

The Catalogue

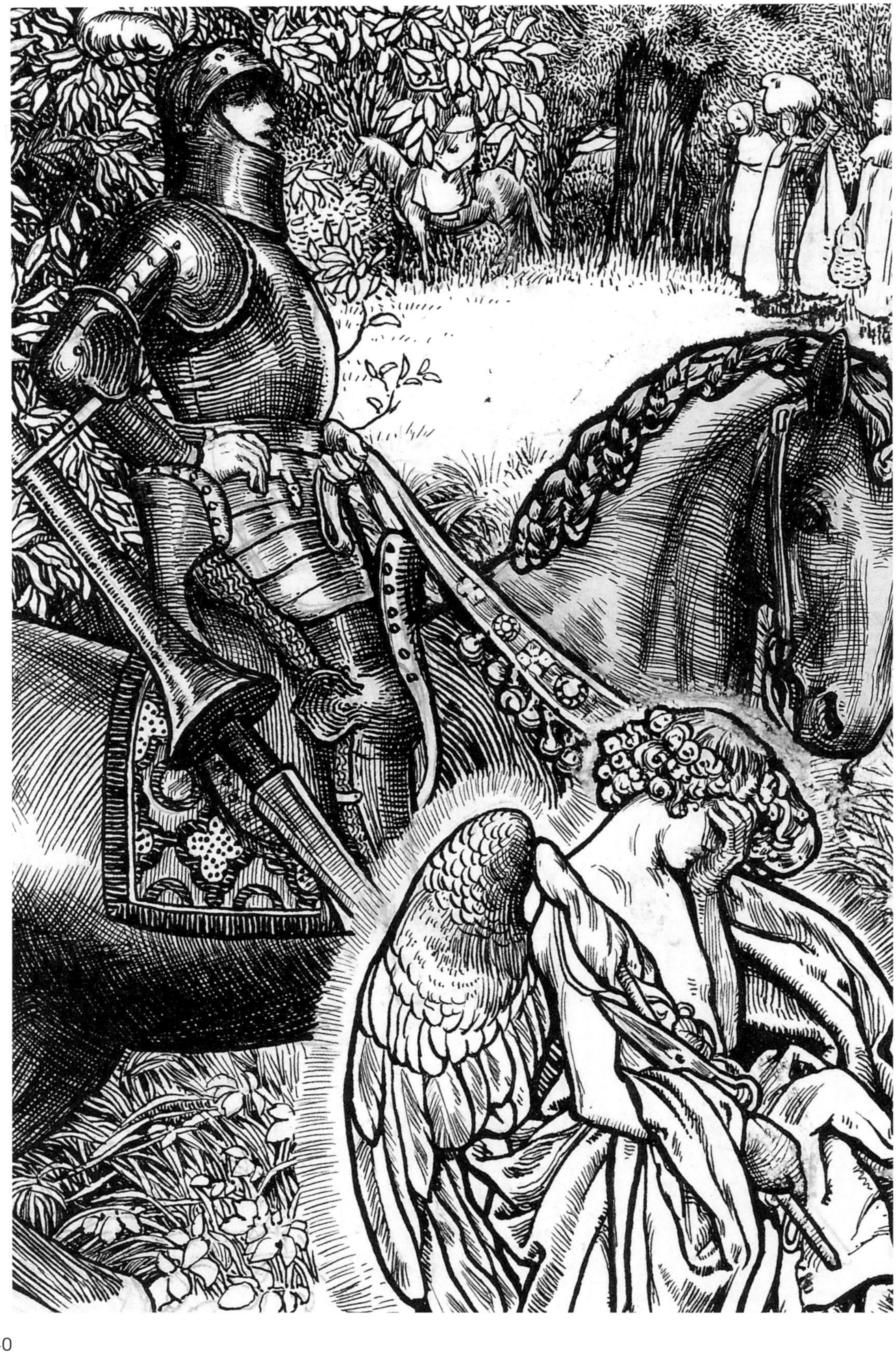

Knight with an Angel of Death, about 1898

Pen/ink over graphite on paper, 36.8 x 23.8 cm

Ashmolean Museum, University of Oxford

The state of this drawing betrays its function, as a design for reproduction on the printed page, most probably to illustrate a poem. Such work would go through several alterations before it was fit for purpose. The gap at the foot of the border has been left for the insertion of a title. Fortescue-Brickdale used this pairing of knight and angel many times: the knight is a noble, if not always successful, figure and the angel his guardian or conscience.

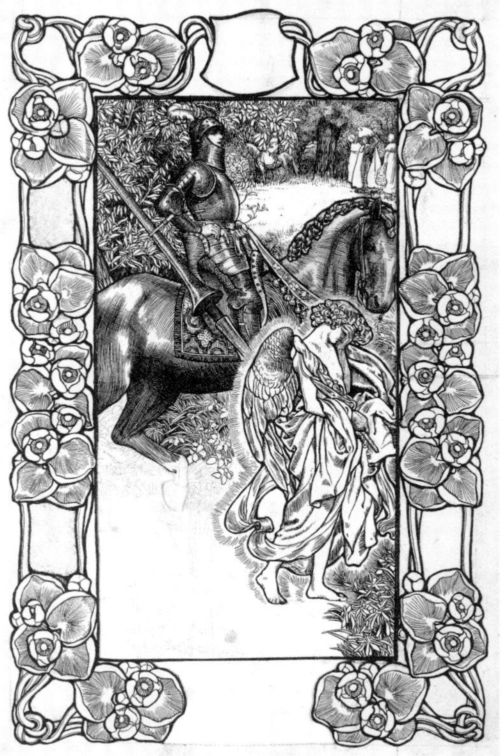

Time the Physician, 1900

Oil on panel, 45.6 x 27.7 cm

Ashmolean Museum, University of Oxford

Fortescue-Brickdale used the figure of Time in several compositions around the turn of the century. Others are *Time and the Maiden* (1899), *Yesterday* (1901), *Today for Me* (1901), *The Three Daughters of Time* (1903), *Love and the Cobbler* (1905) and *Time and Immortality* (1905). In picturing this concept here, the artist was perhaps thinking of Merlin and the Arthurian Knights of the Round Table whom Merlin mentored. While Time is often shown in western art as a force against which human beings must struggle, it is here a benevolent, healing agent which will eventually save the wounded knight.

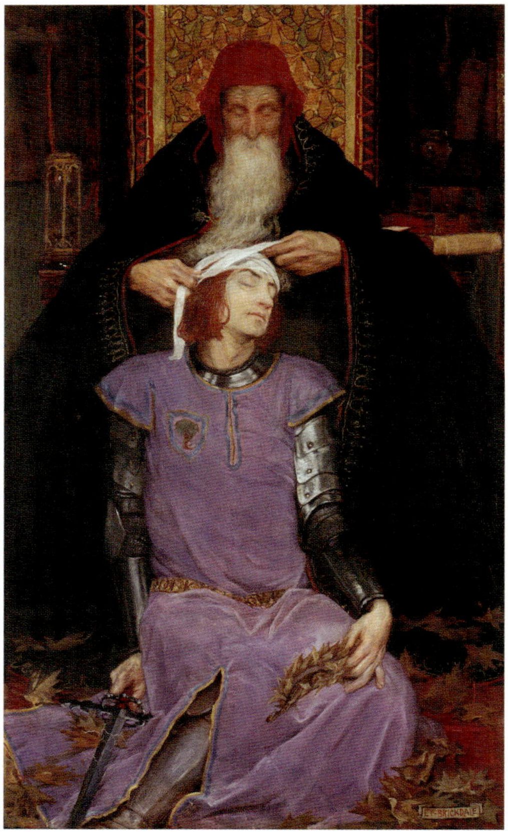

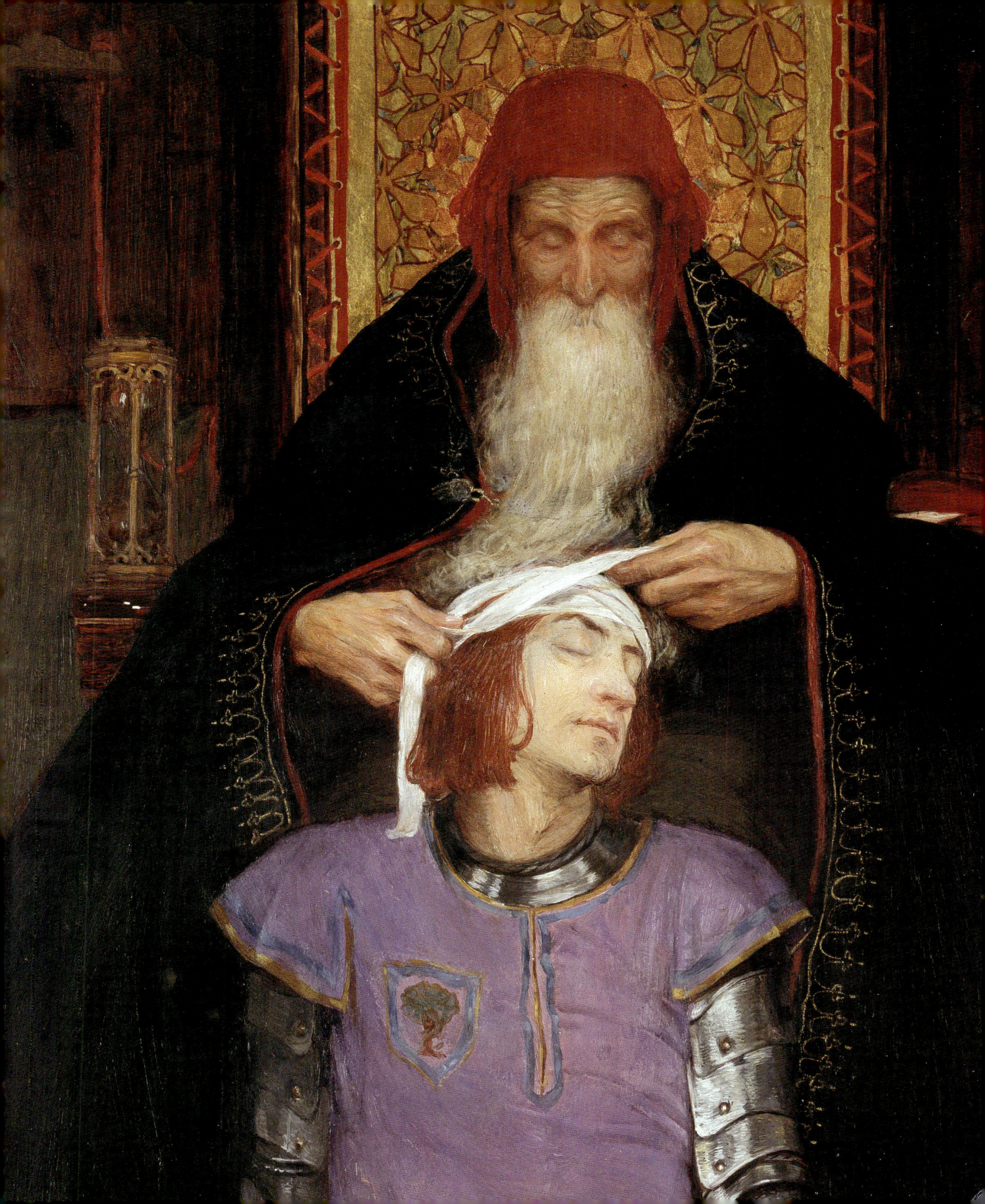

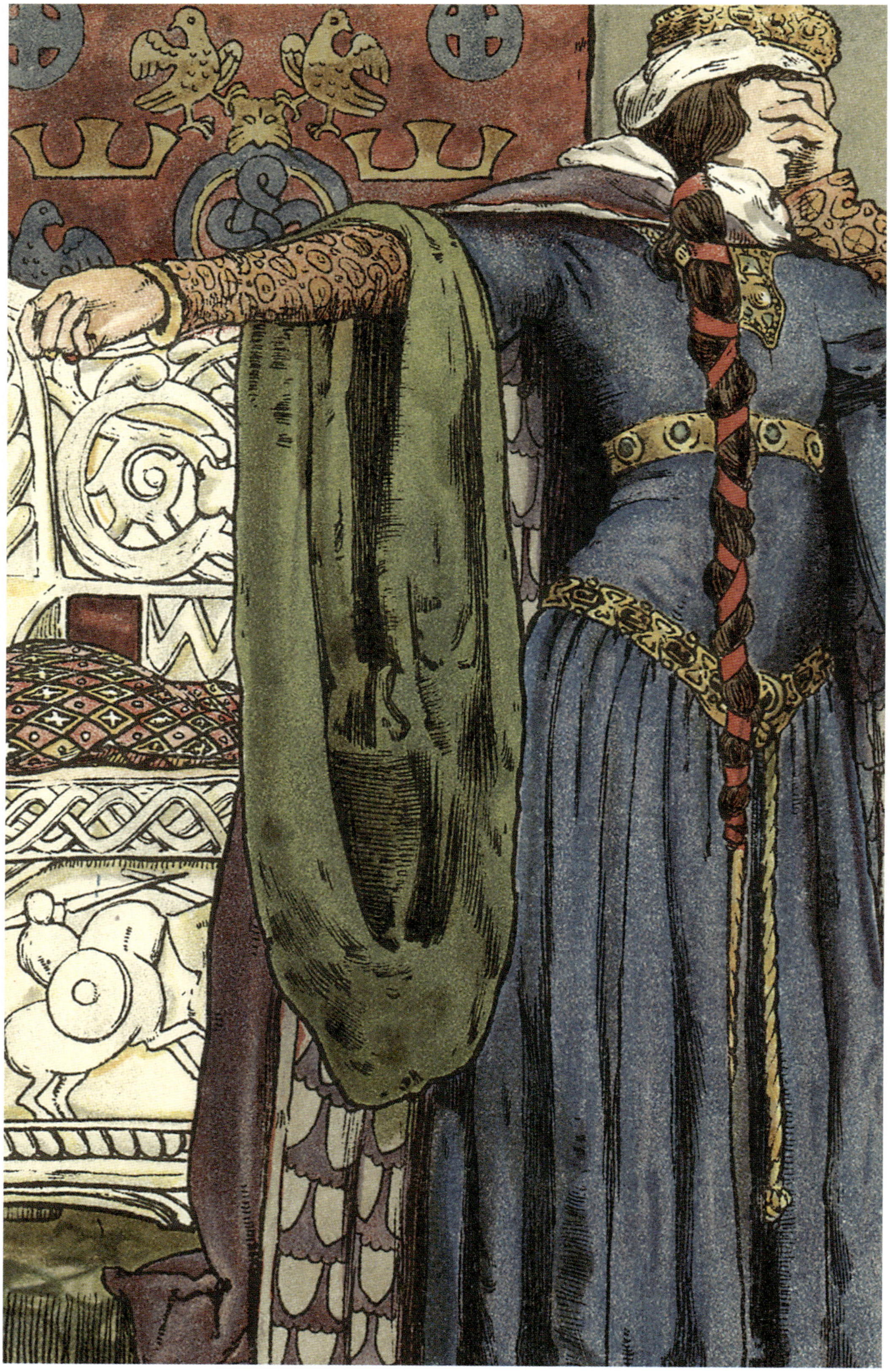

The Complete Works of Shakespeare, Constable, 1901

Birmingham Central Library

This publication was sold serially in 20 volumes beginning in September 1901. Fortescue-Brickdale was one of 12 artists involved. She was allocated *Much Ado about Nothing* (vol. 5, p. 32), *Twelfth Night* (vol. 6, p. 34), *Macbeth* (vol. 14, p. 44) and *Othello* (vol. 15, p. 108). Though this was Fortescue-Brickdale's first attempt at Shakespearean subject-matter, her four designs were among those singled out for praise in most reviews, with the *Studio* reviewer naming particularly the 'Lady Macbeth' plate shown here.

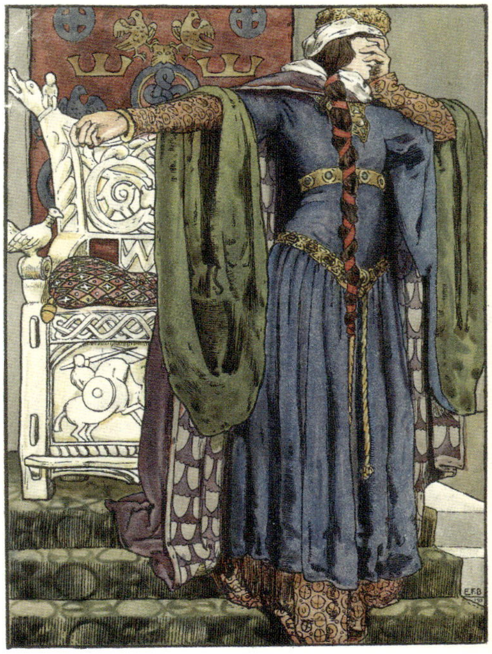

At the Sepulchre,
Pall Mall Magazine, 1901

Fortescue-Brickdale was one of the leading 'black-and-white' artists of the day before she turned to watercolour. This illustration accompanied a poem by Harold Begbie about Jesus rising from the dead on the day after his burial. The figure shown is Mary Magdalene, who has come to anoint the dead body of her Lord - neatly indicated by the little casket in the foreground - but has found his tomb empty. Although the artist generally liked portraying angels, she has chosen to picture the moment just before two angels appear to the weeping Mary and reassure her with a vision of the risen Christ (Book of John, chapter 20).

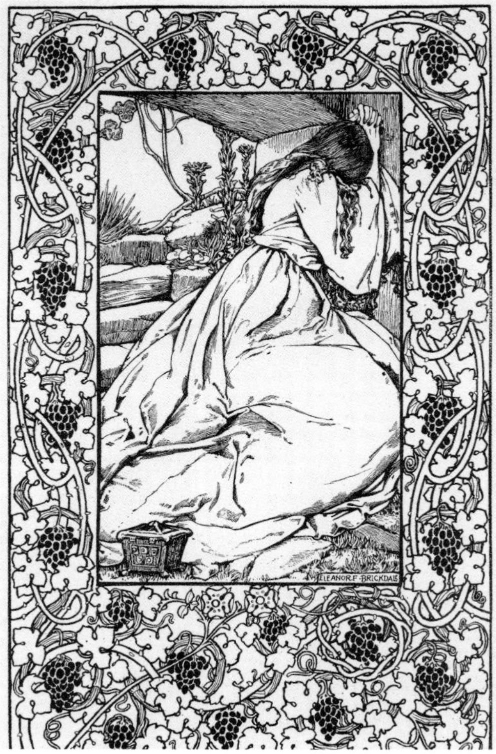

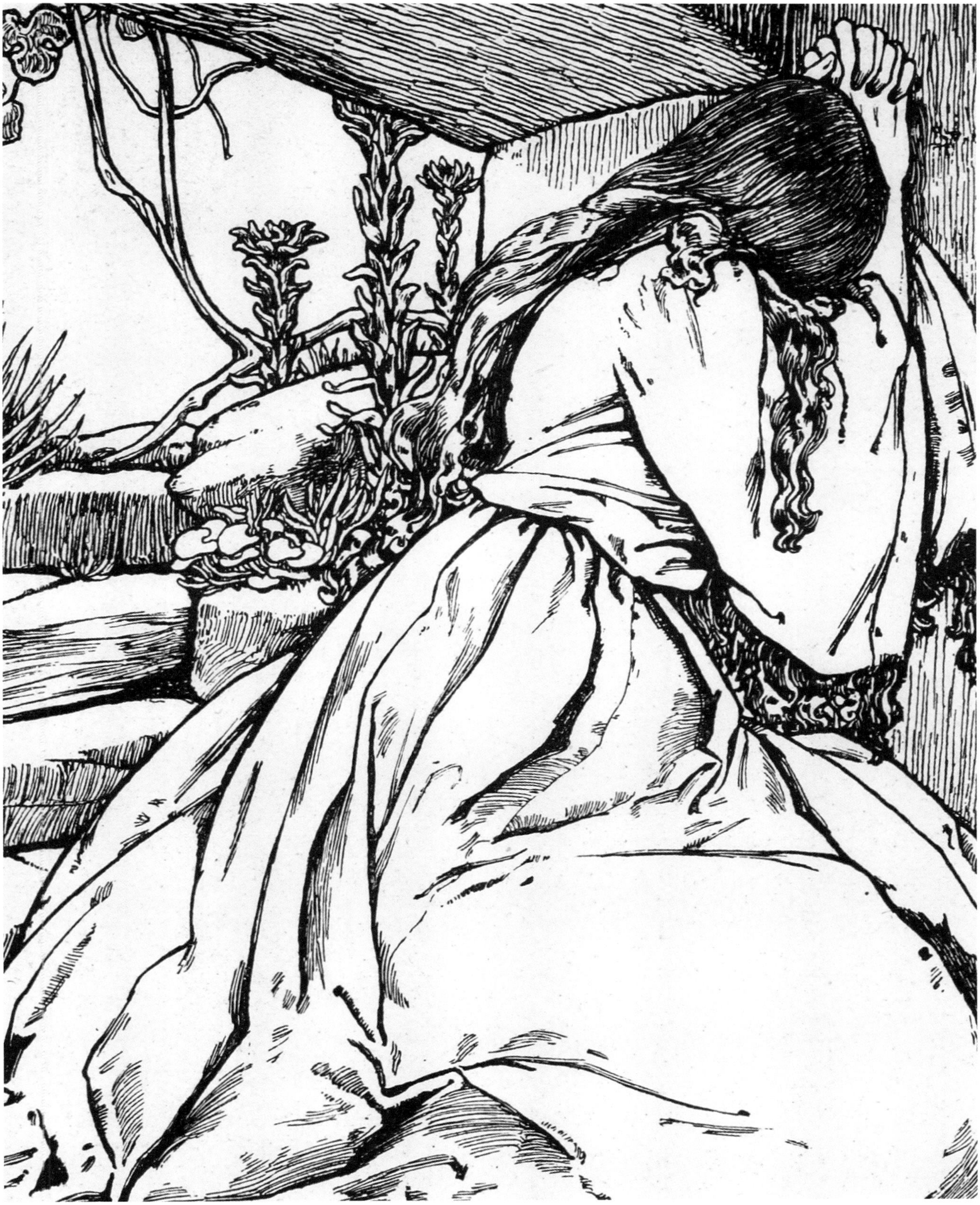

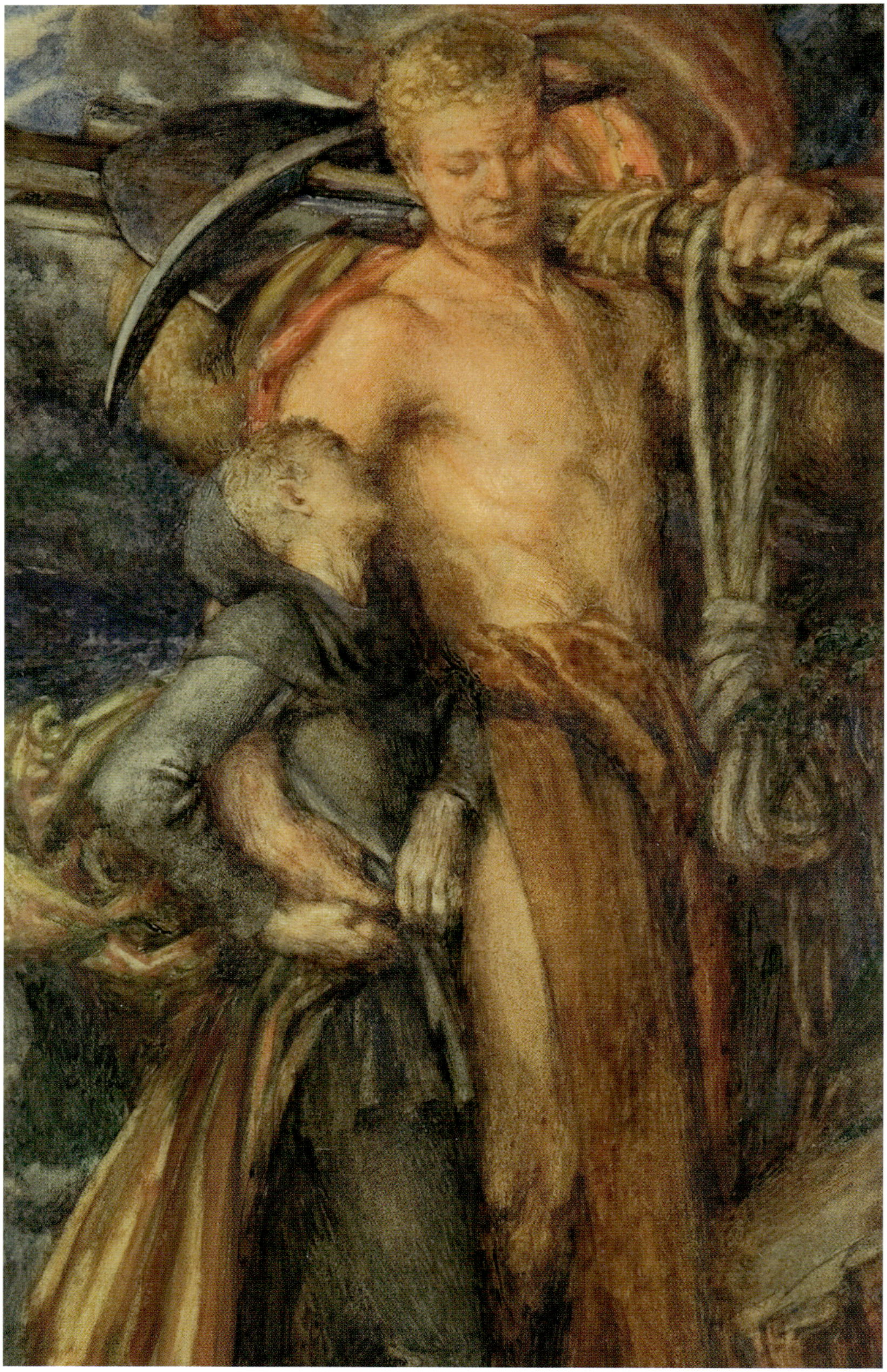

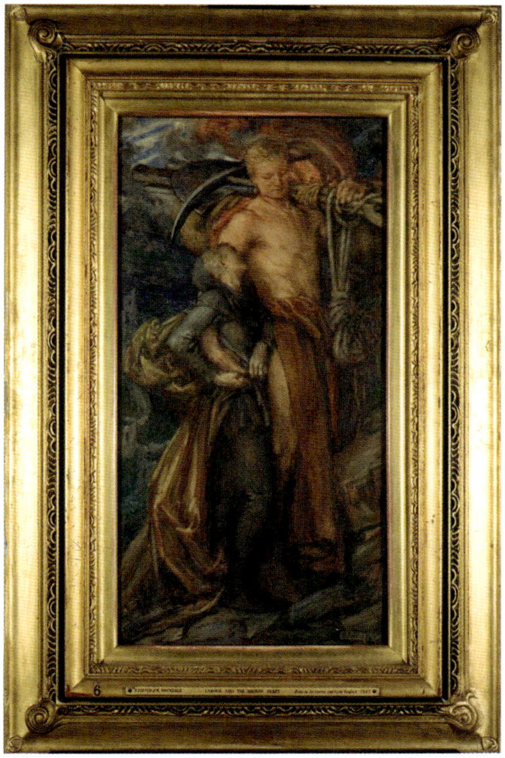

Labour and the Broken Heart,
1904–5

Watercolour, 66 x 35.5 cm

The inspiration of George Frederick Watts, who died in 1904, is apparent here. Watts was especially known for his use of symbolic figures to personify abstract values or virtues, and Fortescue-Brickdale presents a very Wattsian figure of Labour assisting the disappointed figure whose progress through life has been almost brought to a standstill by his broken heart. The ruins of his life and the storm clouds of bitter experience can be seen in the background, but Labour's help is bringing a hint of blue sky. The design of the frame was one of the artist's favourites.

The little Foot-Page, 1905

Oil on canvas, 90.8 x 57 cm

This painting takes its subject from the old Scottish ballad, *Burd Helen*. The heroine is shown cutting off her hair and putting on men's clothing to disguise herself as a page so that she may accompany her sweetheart on his adventures. As the title suggests, she will follow him on foot as a servant while he rides. This familiar plot is given freshness by the artist's focus on the daring and desperate Helen and the intense details of the natural surroundings which enclose her.

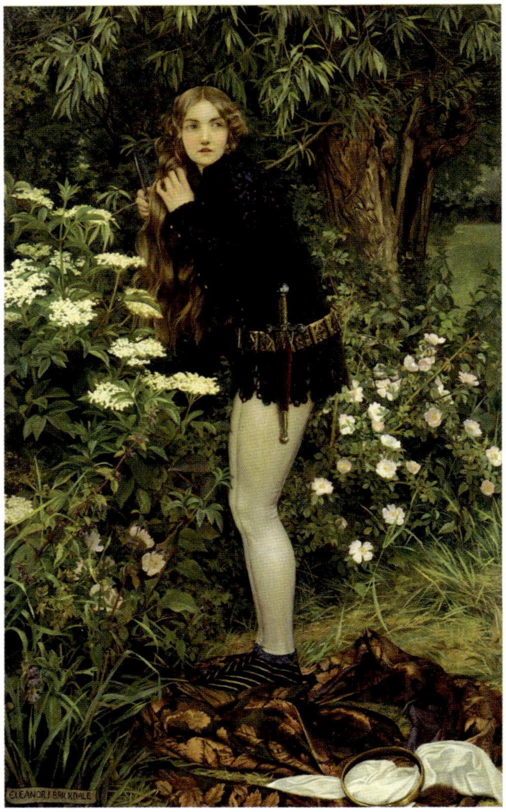

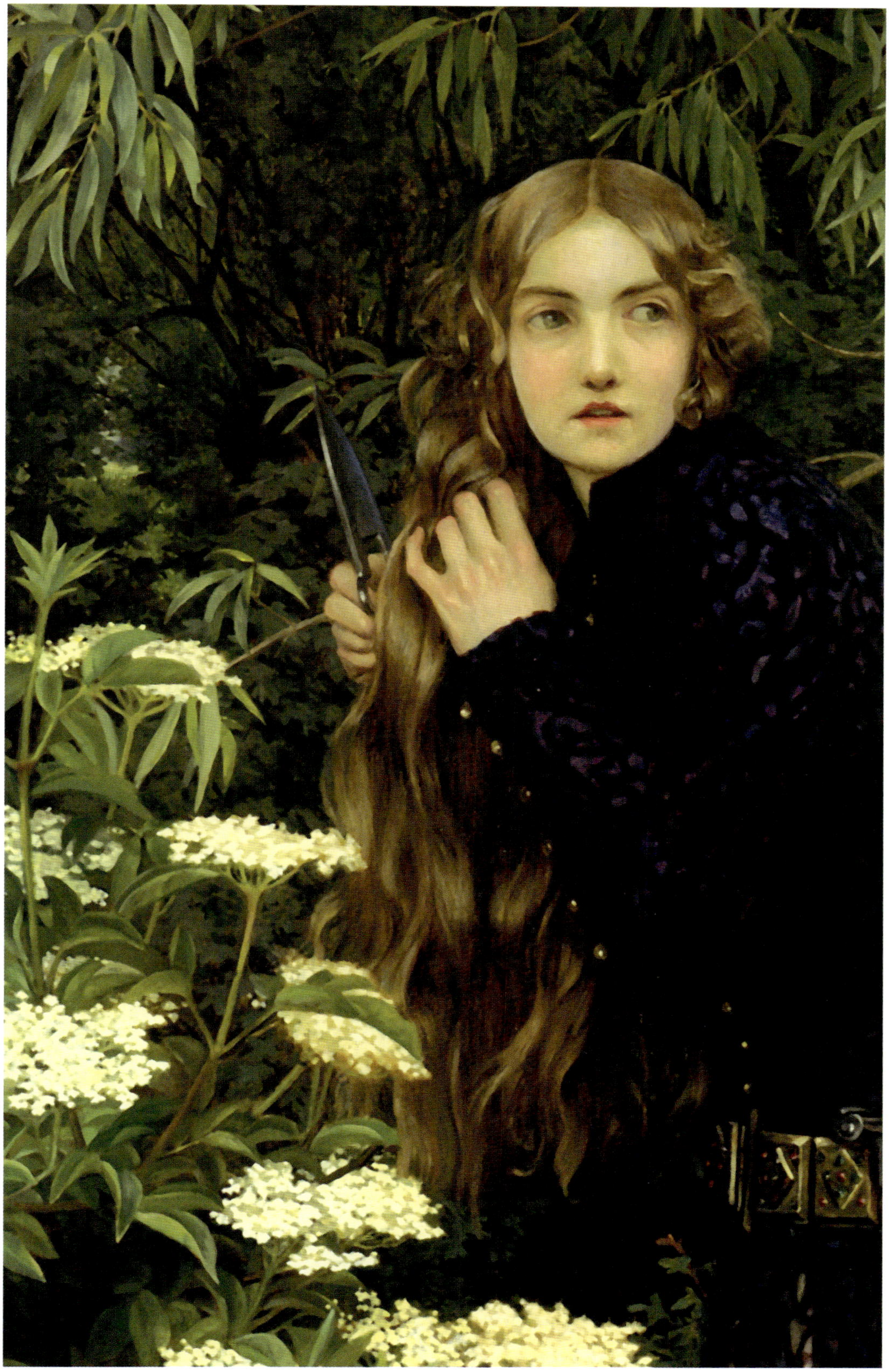

The Statue and the Bust (I did no more while my heart was warm), 1908

Ink, watercolour, body-colour on paper, 36.5 x 25 cm

Ashmolean Museum, University of Oxford

While this drawing is usually identified with Fortescue-Brickdale's illustration of Browning's *Men and Women* (first published 1855), it did not appear in the book. It appears to illustrate the reiterated action of the heroine, looking out to the town square to get a glimpse of her lover, the Duke, whenever he passes. Brickdale was reproached by critics for not respecting the plots of Browning's poems, and certainly here the toddler is her own invention, perhaps to emphasise that in yearning after the Duke, the heroine betrays her duties as a wife.

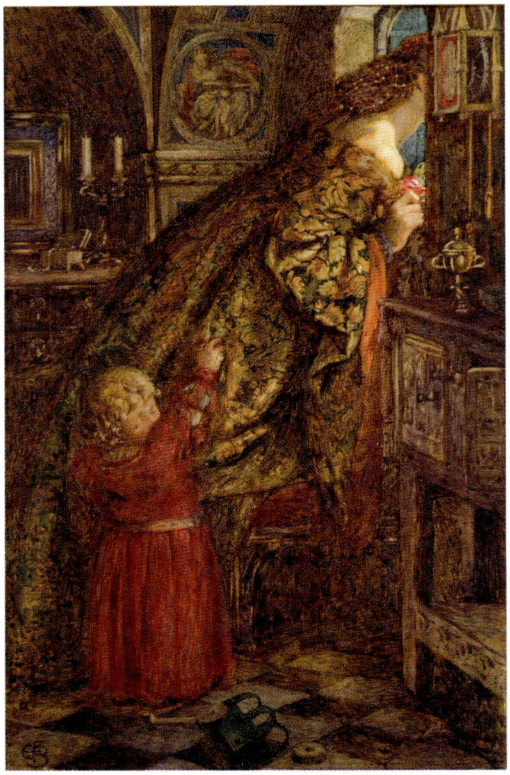

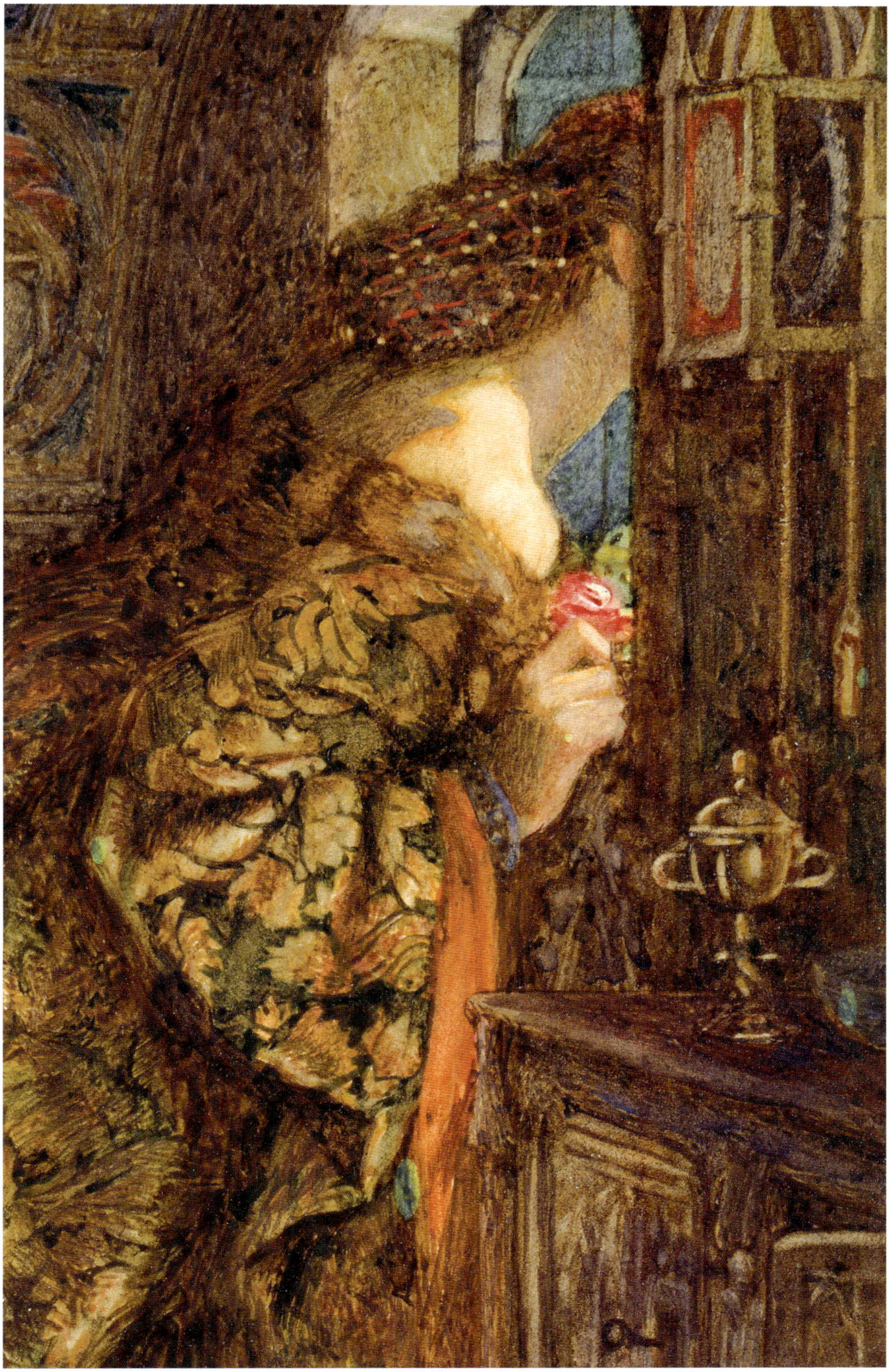

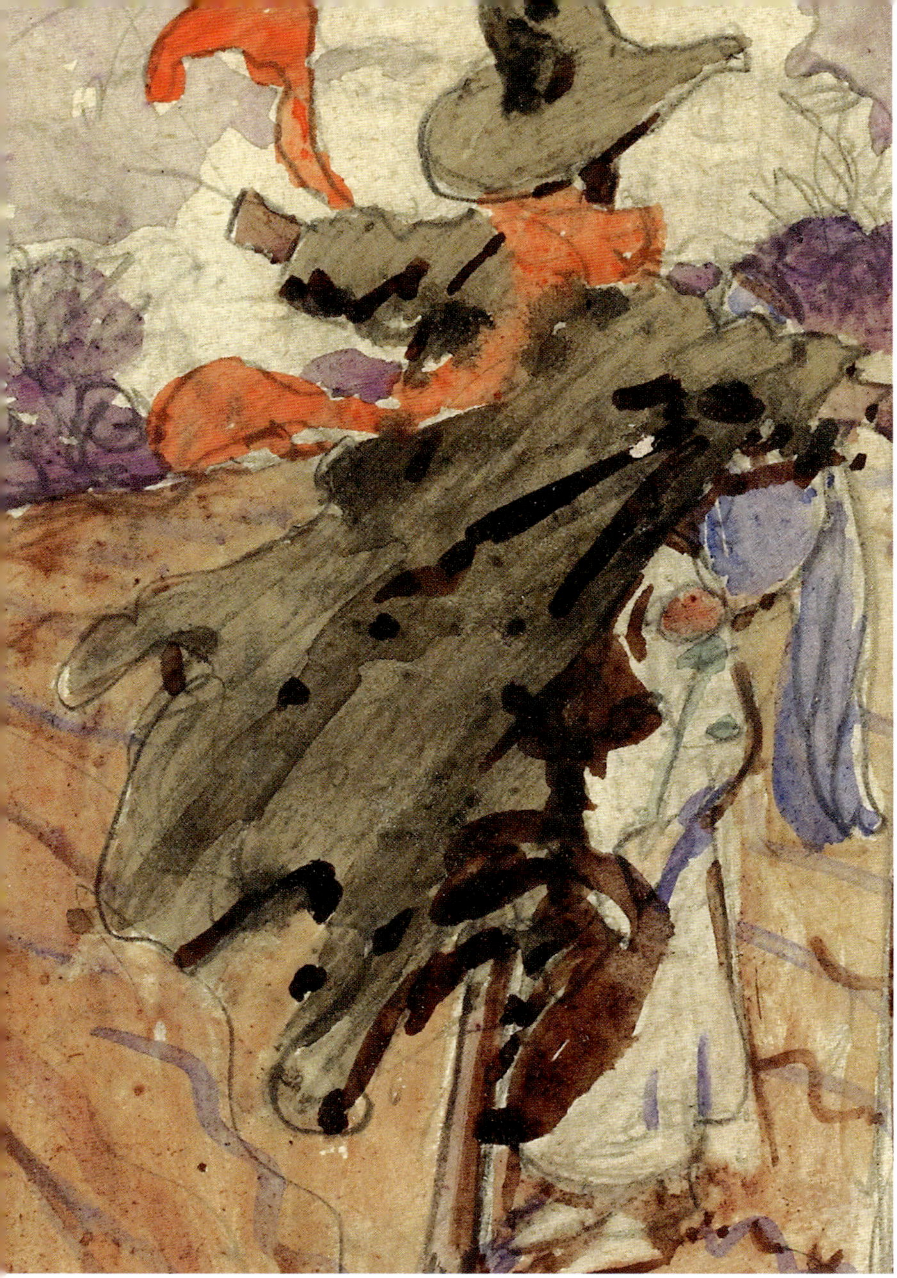

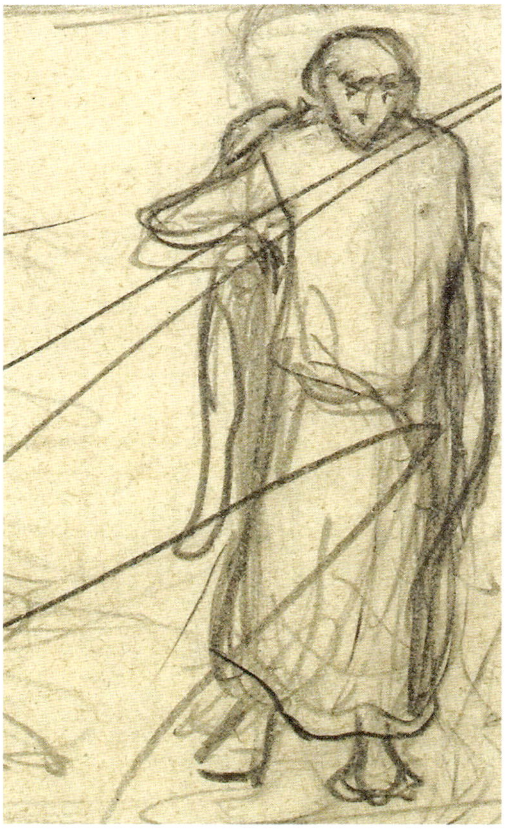

Two studies for *The World and what it fears*, 1908

Graphite, watercolour on paper, 22.5 x 17.3 cm

Ashmolean Museum, University of Oxford

Fortescue-Brickdale's treatment of Browning's poem *Respectability*, for the illustrated edition of *Men and Women*, typifies the fancifulness that led to her being criticised for failing to honour the poet's intention. Certainly, there is no sign here of the contemporary romantic couple wandering the streets of Paris whom Browning conjures up in his verse. Instead, the artist uses her favourite figure of an angelic Love, encountering the scarecrow of public opinion. The open field and suggestion of a cold wind – drawn to the viewer's attention by the red scarf of the scarecrow – emphasise Love's vulnerability.

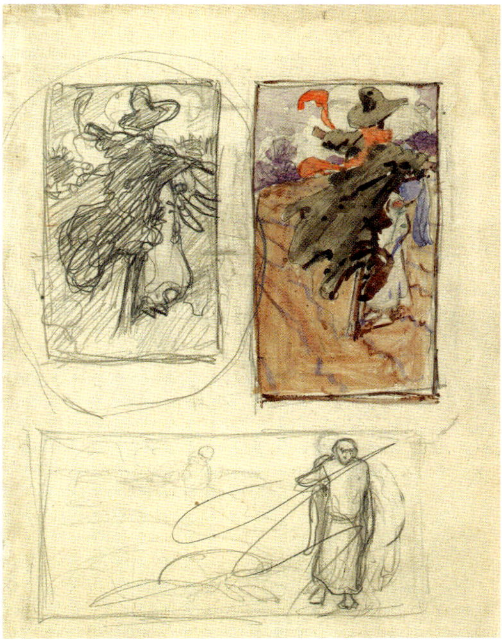

Sketch for *The World and what it fears*, 1908

Pastels on paper, 46.9 x 26.6 cm

Ashmolean Museum, University of Oxford

As the idea is developed, certain aspects of the picture change to convey the message or story more effectively. The menace of the scarecrow is heightened as the artist works up the colour scheme of the composition, while Love's yellow hair and touches of pink in feet and wings increase its decorative beauty. The bright red rose held away from itself by Love, as if to protect it from the stifling embrace of public opinion, adds to Love's preciousness. The wonderful dynamism of the chalks infuses the entire encounter with greater emotion.

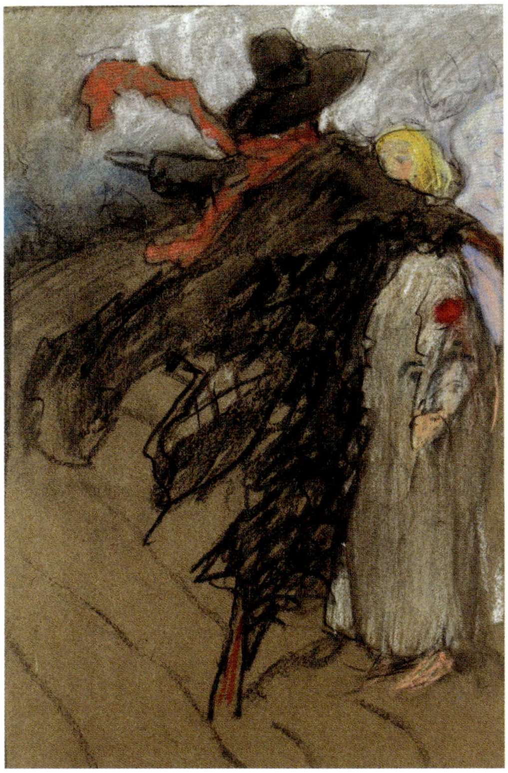

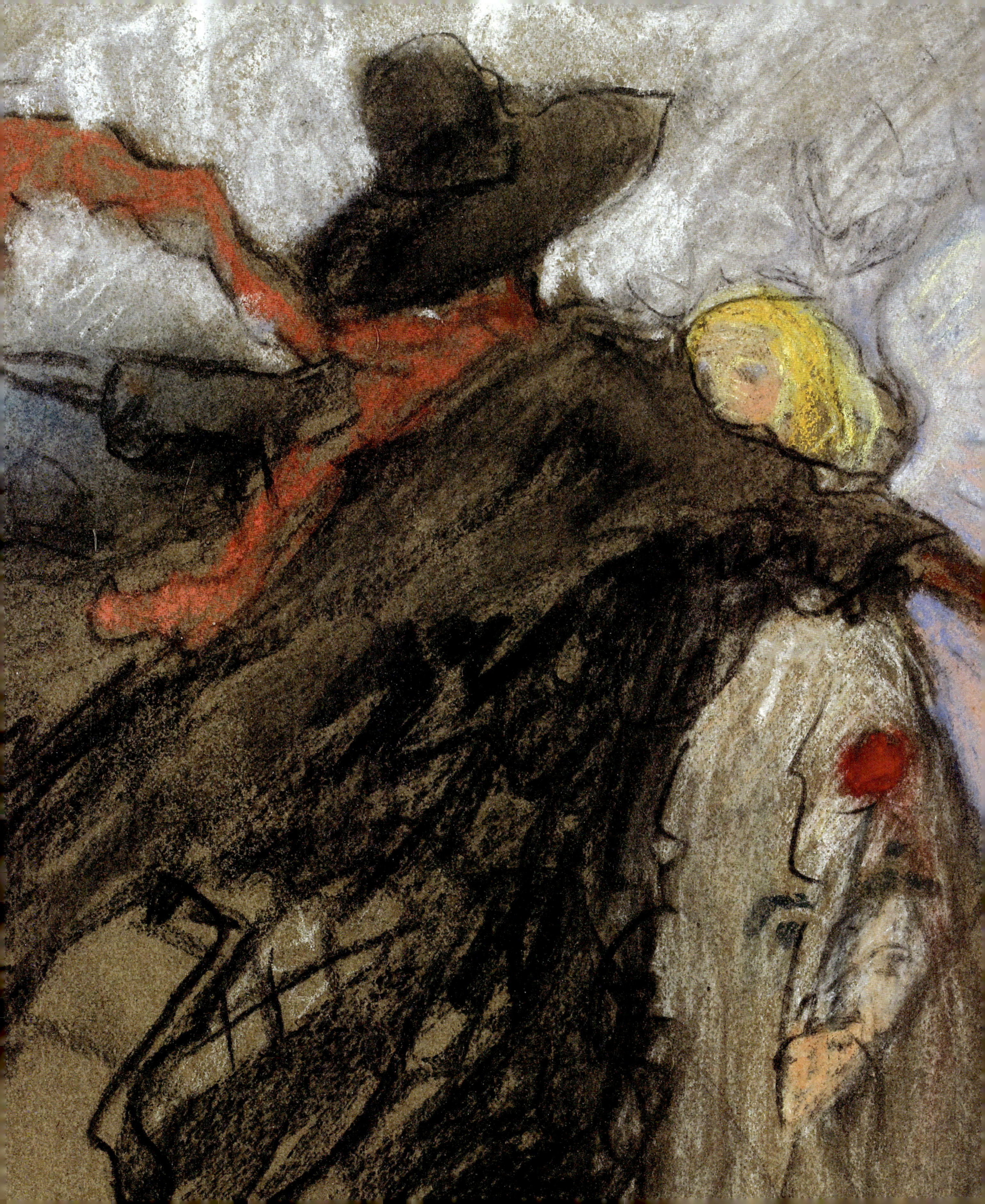

Robert Browning, *Pippa passes and Men and Women*, illustrated by Eleanor F. Brickdale, Chatto and Windus, 1908

In the design as it eventually appeared in the book, the positions of Love and the scarecrow have changed markedly. Now Love – whose angelic night dress has been exchanged for a richer robe – is half hidden by the scarecrow of public opinion; its other-worldly charm partially obscured by dull respectability, flapping noisily in the wind. That it is cabbages – the most mundane of crops – that the scarecrow would protect shows the artist's whimsy. Who, she asks, would value a whole field of cabbages more than a single rose offered by Love?

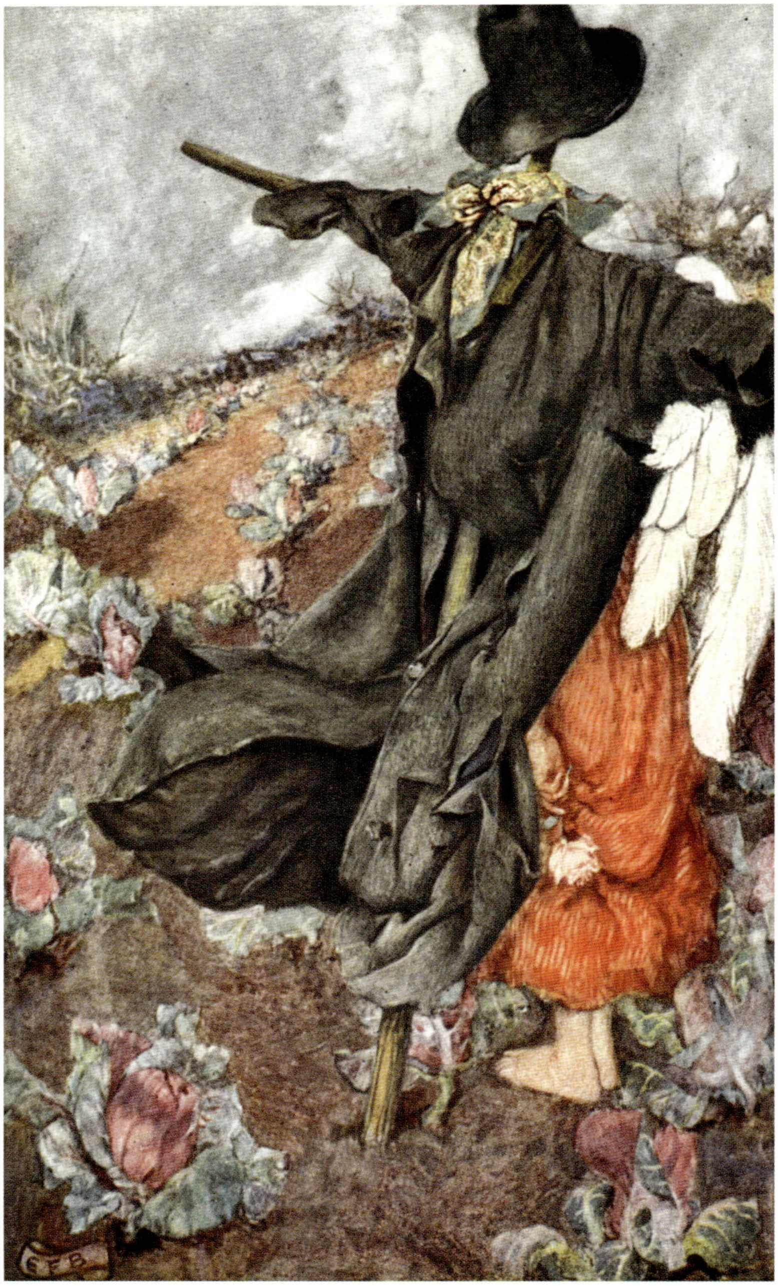

If one could have that Little Head of hers, 1909

Watercolour, body-colour, gold on paper, 31.8 x 19 cm

Photograph reproduced with the kind permission of The Russell-Cotes Art Gallery & Museum BORGM 00360

Robert Browning was celebrating 'Tuscan' (or Florentine) painting in the poem that this design accompanies in the 1909 edition of his *Dramatis Personae and Dramatic Romances and Lyrics* that Fortescue-Brickdale illustrated. In recognition of this, the artist has drawn on portraits by Renaissance artists seen on her several visits to Italy. As well as recalling her own earlier Browning subject, *My last Duchess* (1904–5), this design bears a particular resemblance to a supposed portrait of Beatrice d'Este by Leonardo's assistant, Giovanni Ambrogio de Predis, evoked again later in *The Forerunner* (1920).

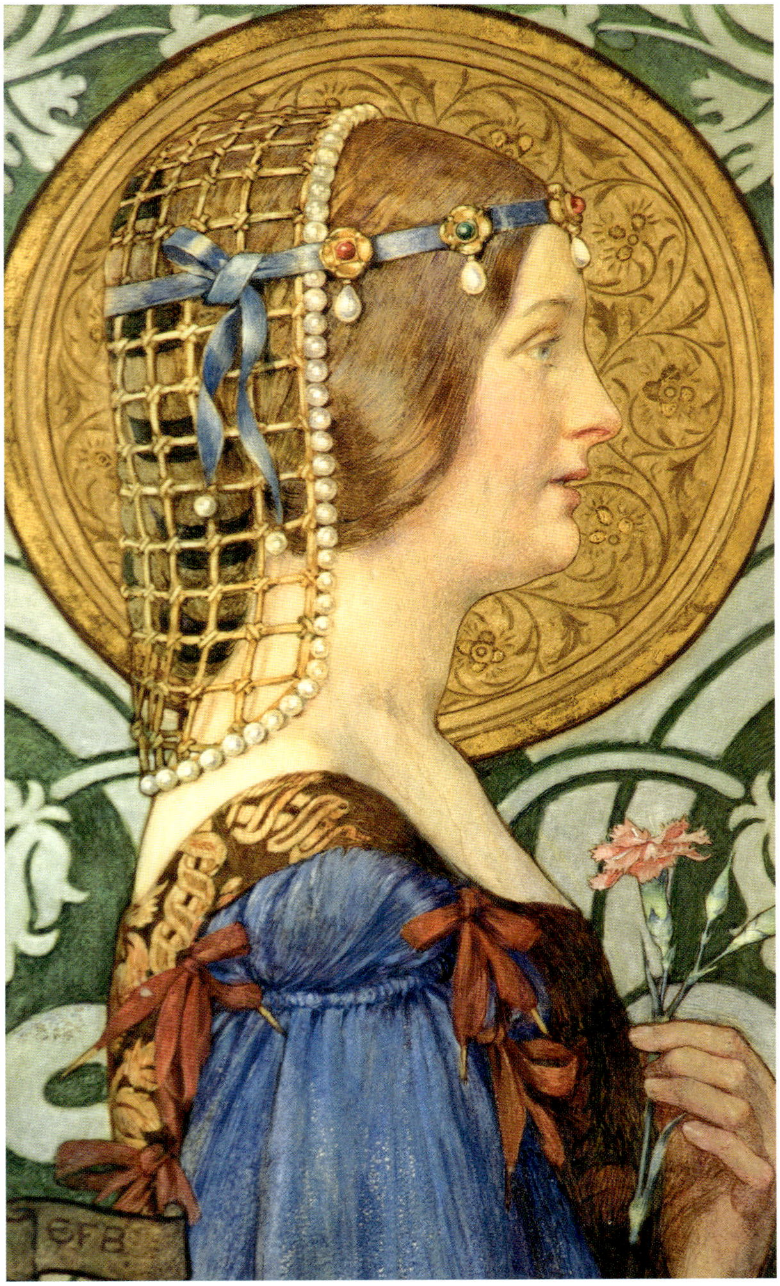

Robert Browning, *Dramatis Personae and Dramatic and Romantic Lyrics*, illustrated by Eleanor Fortescue-Brickdale, Chatto and Windus, 1909

Of the ten plates in this book, '*Is she not pure gold, my mistress?*' stands out for its contemporaneity. Compositionally, the heroine is a modern counterpart to Burd Helen (*The little Foot-Page*, 1905), surrounded but not overwhelmed by nature, and looking confidently out of the picture-space. While she recalls the female figures of the founding Pre-Raphaelite, JE Millais, in her address to the viewer, she seems much more a woman of Fortescue-Brickdale's time.

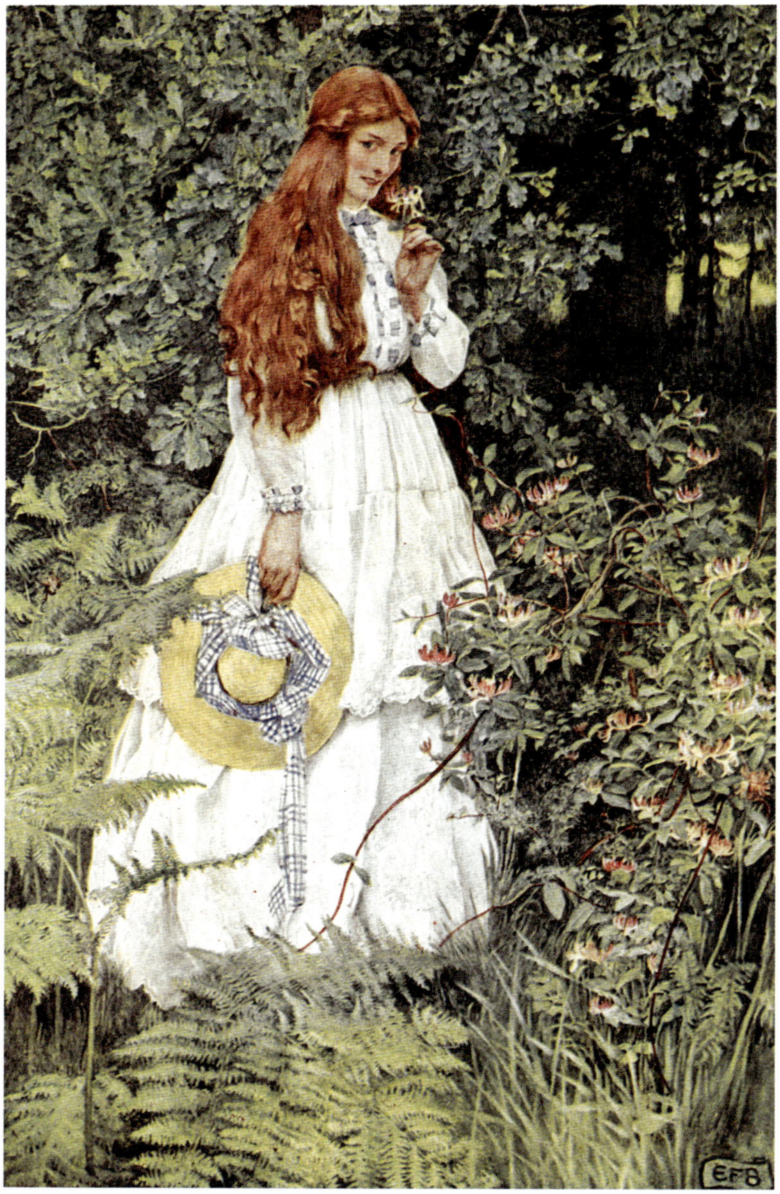

HJ Wright and WP Wright, *Beautiful Flowers and How to Grow Them*, TC and EC Jack, 1909

This publication was issued in 17 parts, containing 100 colour plates by ten artists. Fortescue-Brickdale's contributions, noted by several reviewers, were given prominence by being used for the frontispiece of volume 1 and the covers of parts 2 and 4. She has emphasised the inherent beauty of her floral subjects by presenting them without any background matter – a bolder approach than that adopted by most of the other contributors. Occasional studies of flowers occur throughout Fortescue-Brickdale's work, highlighting her Pre-Raphaelite love of nature for its own sake.

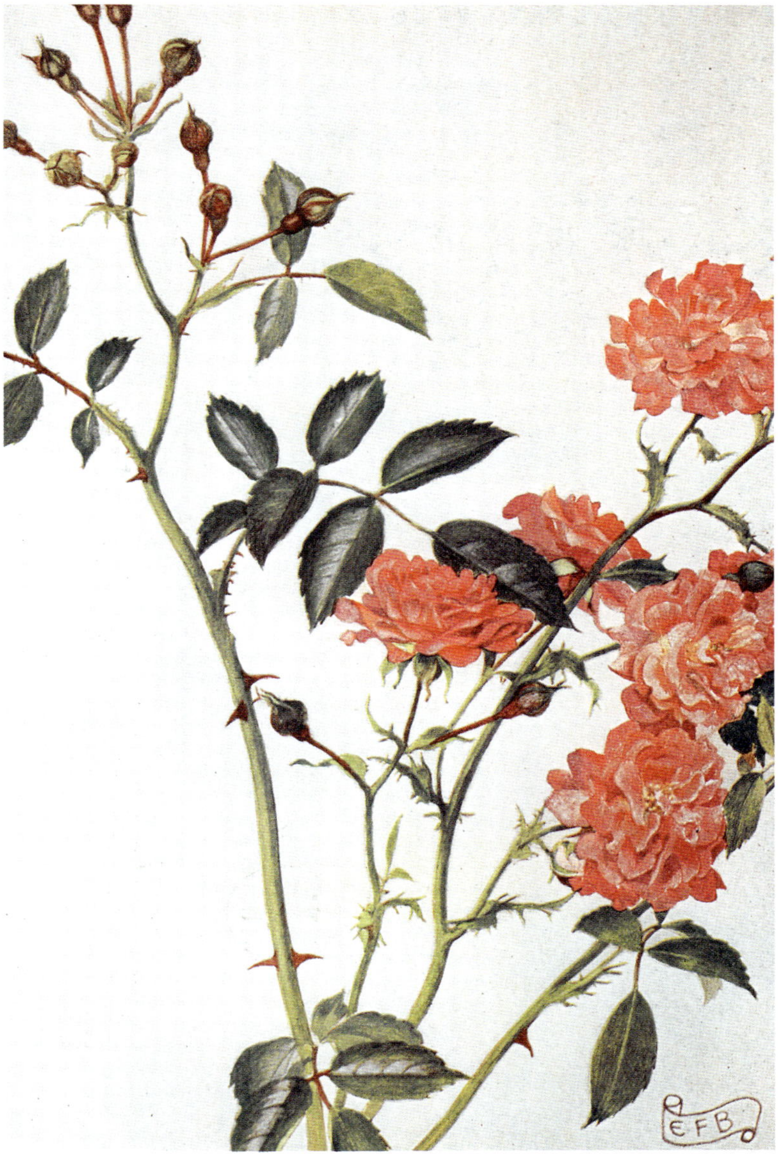

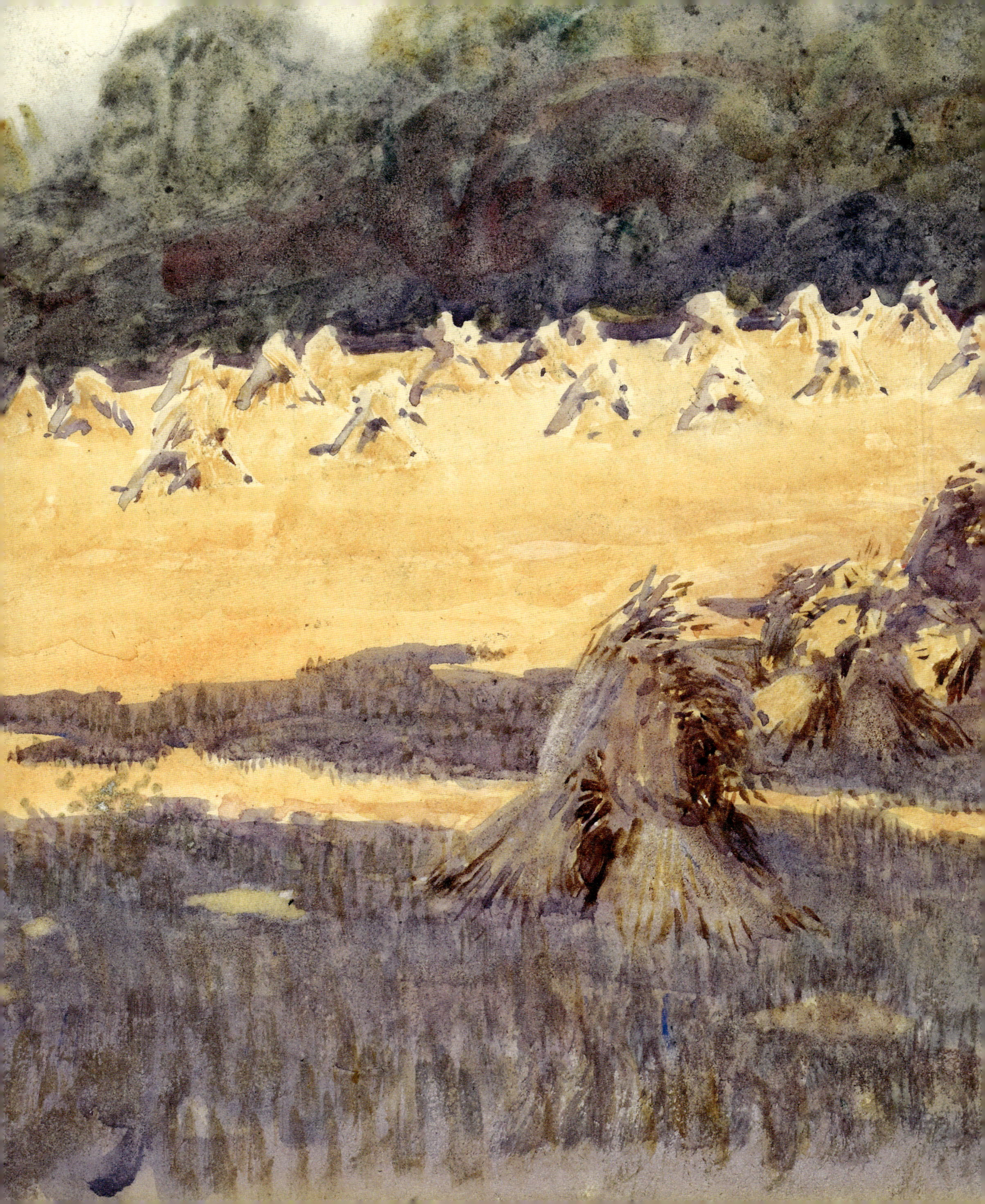

Autumn Fields, Condover, undated

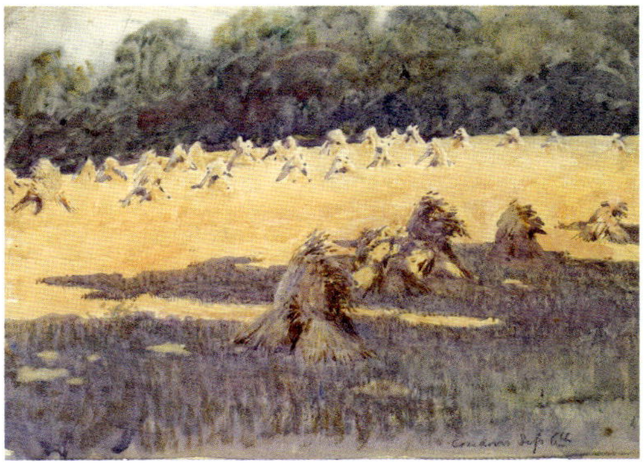

Watercolour on paper, 19.1 x 26 cm

Ashmolean Museum, University of Oxford

Fortescue-Brickdale was always on the lookout for useful bits of background or scenery, and she often found these at the provincial homes of her friends and patrons. Condover Hall, a few miles south of Shrewsbury, known as the grandest Elizabethan house in Shropshire, belonged to Edward Fielden MP and his wife Maisie Theed, and diary entries and photographs show that Fortescue-Brickdale was a visitor there over many years. A friend noted in 1941, "Bricky is sorry that the Fieldens no longer live at Condover as she loved the place..." At least one other watercolour by the artist referring to Condover exists, made in 1919.

The rusty Knight (Yniol's rusted arms), 1910–11

Watercolour on paper, 44.2 x 25.6 cm

In the third of the five plates illustrating Enid's story in Tennyson's *Idylls of the King*, she is shown with the knight Geraint, whom she later marries. He has borrowed a suit of armour from her father Yniol, in order to challenge Enid's other suitor on the tournament field. A somewhat flawed hero, after his marriage Geraint's initial 'princely' character gives way to possessiveness and mistrust. The artist has surely intended to mock him slightly here, peeking apprehensively out of his ill-fitting armour and mounted immobile on his outsize horse as he proceeds towards the joust to prove his valour.

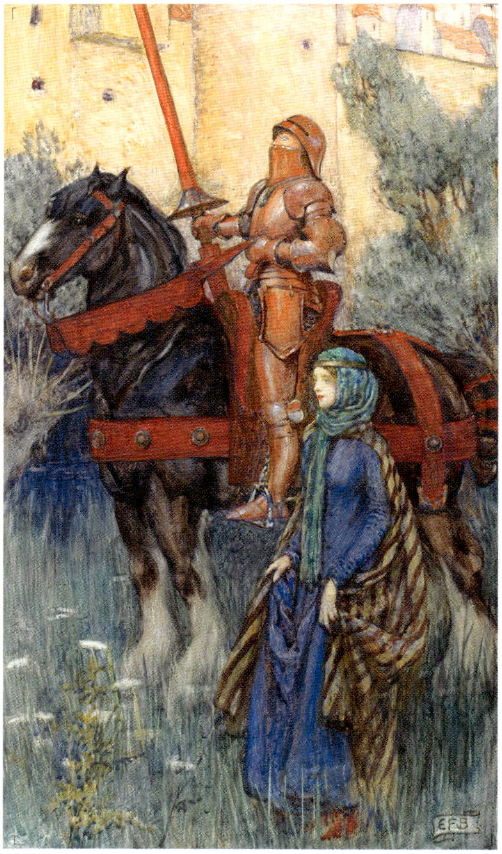

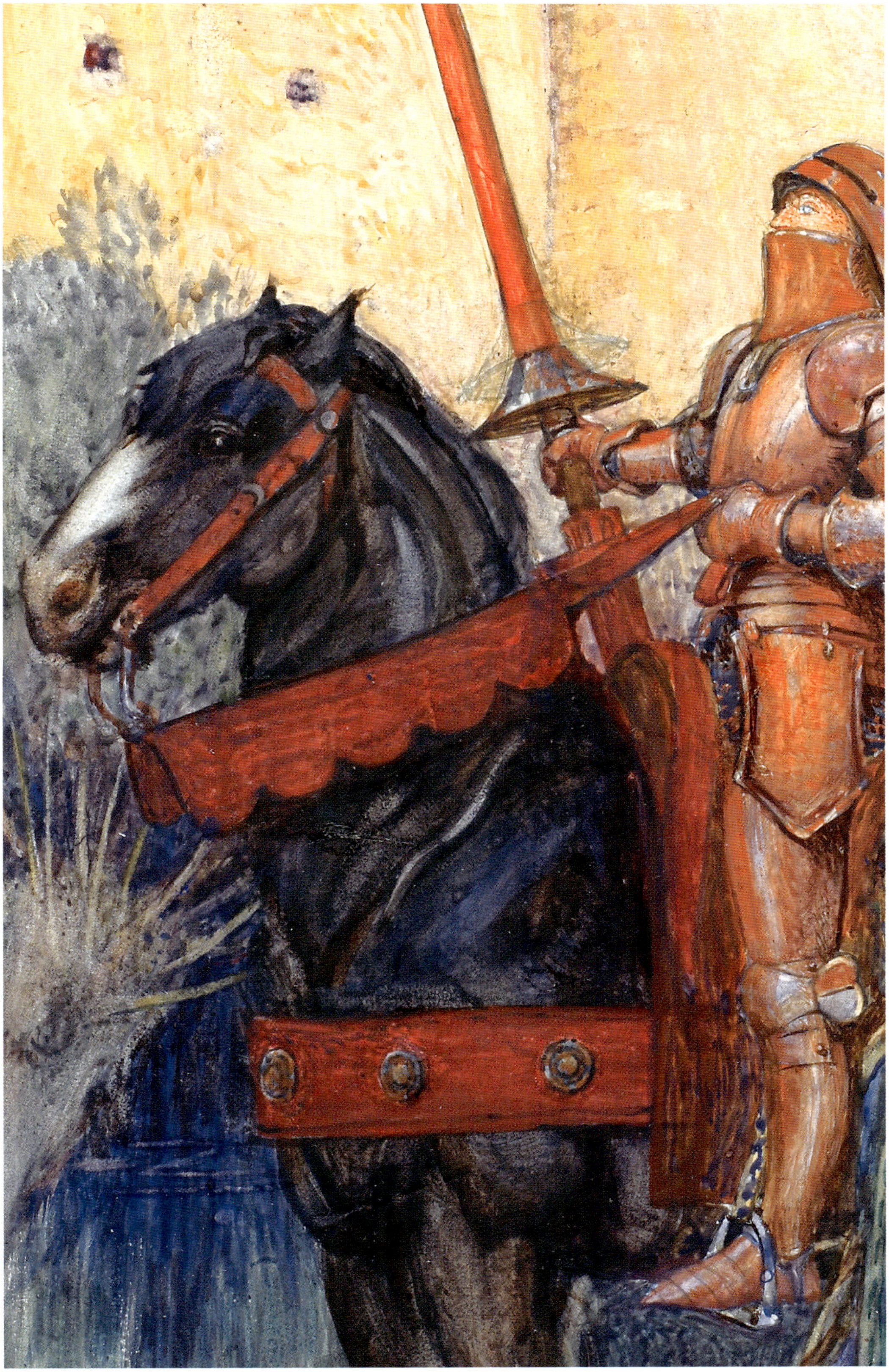

Merlin and Vivien, 1910-11

Watercolour on paper, 44.2 x 25.6 cm

Reproduced with kind permission of Nicholas Byam Shaw and the Bridgeman Art Library

Vivien, also known as Nimue, is one of Tennyson's bad women. Ambitious and scheming, she competes with men for power and influence. In this, the second of the four plates in the book dedicated to her story, she shows her villainy. Intent on getting Merlin, the magician of King Arthur's court, to share his magic with her, she attempts to seduce him with a love-song. The artist reveals Vivien's character by her serpentine body, the snake-like sheen of her dress and her coquettish play with the old man's beard. Fifteen pages later, her success in this perfidious scheme is illustrated by the sight of Merlin at the foot of this same tree, alone and bereft of his magic powers, a broken man.

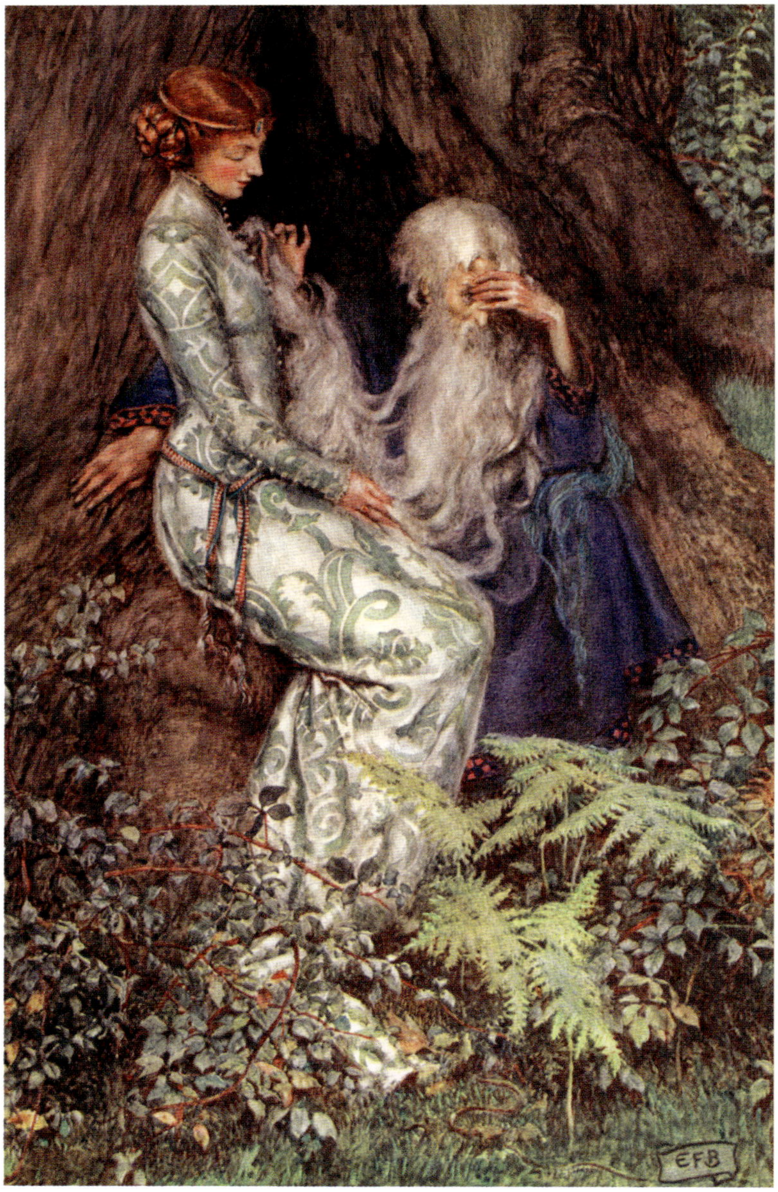

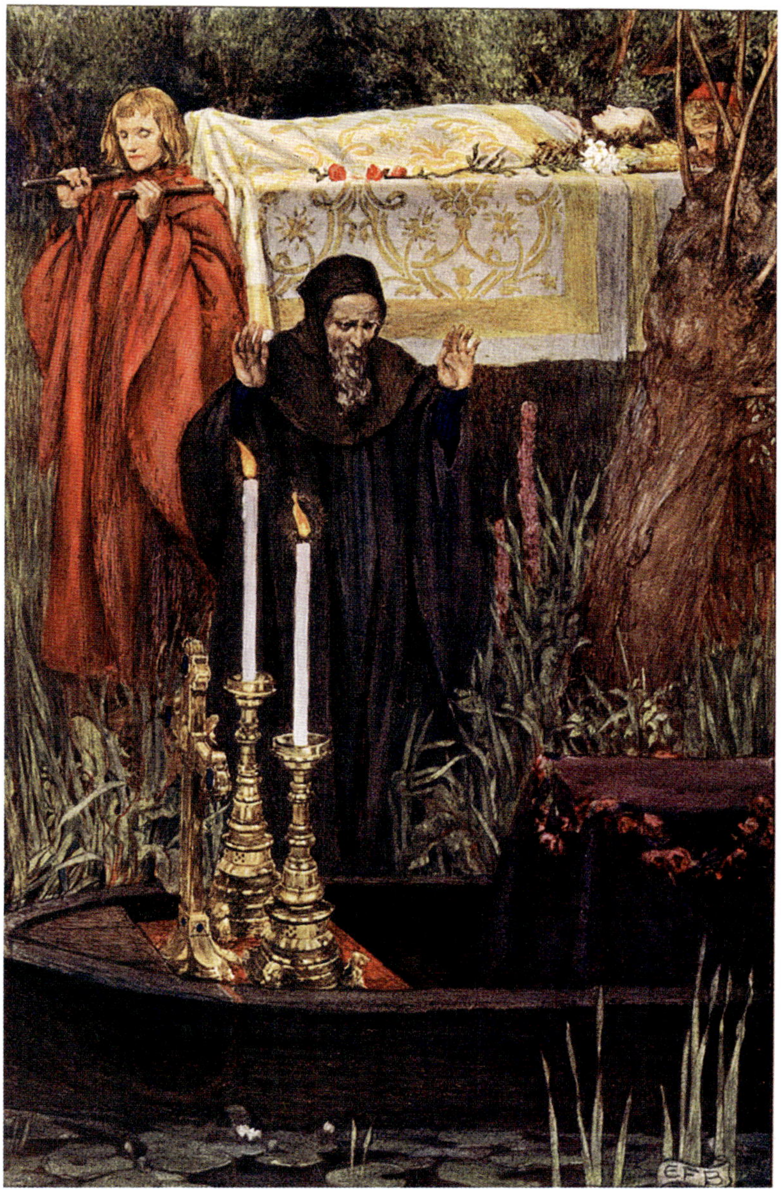

The Passing of Elaine, 1910–11

Watercolour on paper, 45 x 26 cm

Reproduced with kind permission of Julia Elton and the Bridgeman Art Library

Of the four women who are the subjects of Fortescue-Brickdale's edition of Tennyson's *Idylls*, Elaine is given the most appealing story. As a naïve and affectionate girl, sometimes referred to as the Lily Maid of Astolat, she falls in love with the glamorous knight, Lancelot, who has no romantic feeling for her. After a sequence of disappointments, she dies of a broken heart: the subject of this, the fourth of the five plates in the book illustrating her story. She has ordered "a chariot-bier to take me to the river" and a barge, "clothed in black", upon which she will take her last journey down the river to Arthur's court in the castle at Camelot.

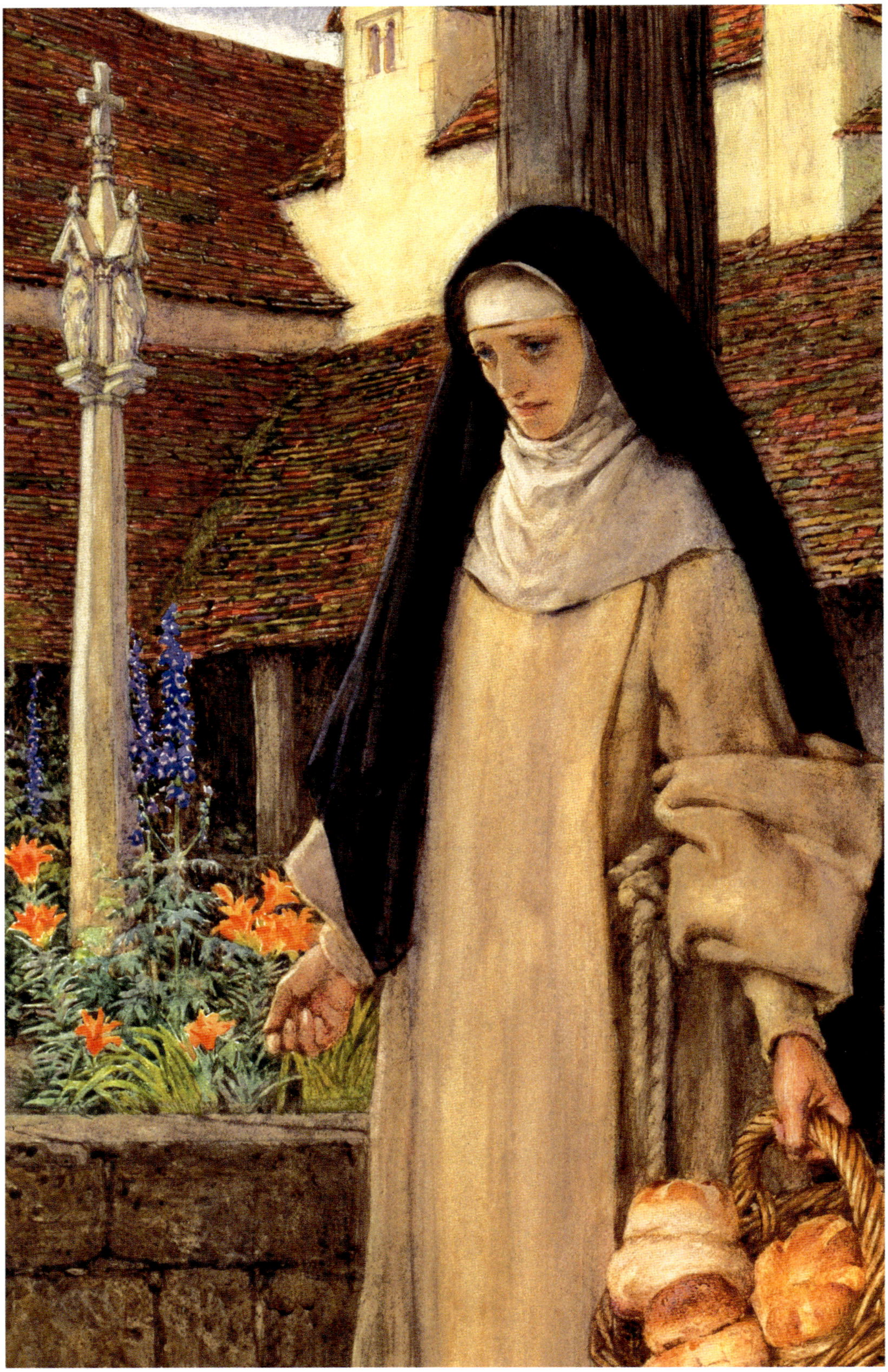

Guinevere (The sombre close of that voluptuous day), 1910–11

Watercolour on paper, 45.3 x 26.6 cm

© Birmingham Museums & Art Gallery

Of the six plates treating Guinevere, this is the last, and the final illustration in the book. After the ultimate failure of her marriage to Arthur and romance with his first knight, Lancelot, Tennyson has the Queen embrace a life of humility, almost of anonymity. The artist shows her at the repetitive work of serving others and contributing to the routine maintenance of the convent's daily life. The absolute quiet and stillness of the setting neatly emphasise the contrast between this life and that which Guinevere enjoyed in her heyday.

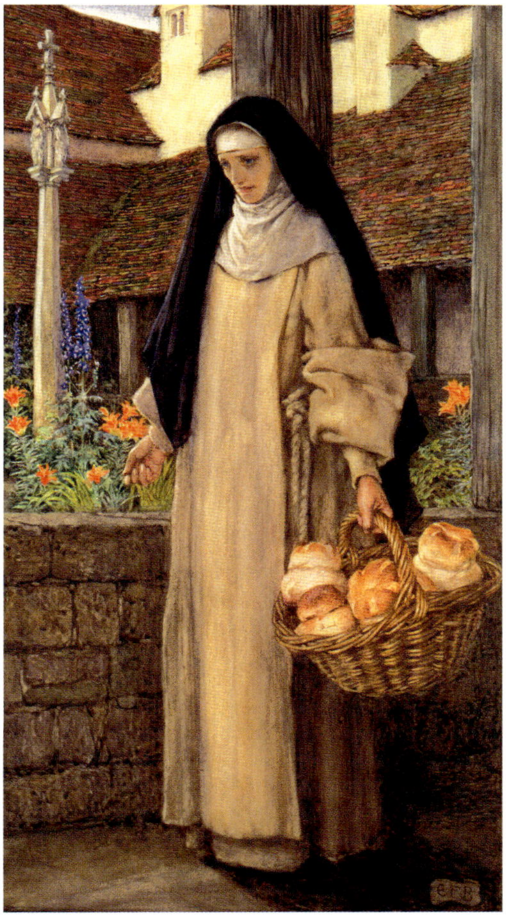

Portrait of Winifred Roberts, 1913

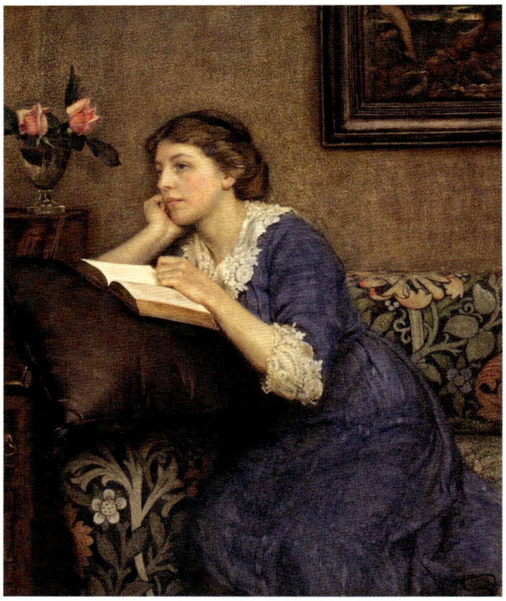

Watercolour, ink on paper, 52.4 x 44.6 cm

Tullie House Museum and Art Gallery Trust

Winifred Roberts (1893-1981) studied in about 1910-1914 at the Byam Shaw School of Art, where Fortescue-Brickdale taught. This portrait, commissioned by the sitter's grandmother Rosalind Howard, celebrates the taste for the Pre-Raphaelite style that all three women shared. This is signalled in Roberts' dress, in the couch covered in a Morris and Company fabric, and in the presence at top right of Byam Shaw's painting *Cupid driving the Lovers*. Though she was a great admirer of her teacher Byam Shaw, when Roberts became a well-known artist herself it was as a modern painter of landscapes and still lifes, under her married name of Nicholson (the Tate owns several of her works).

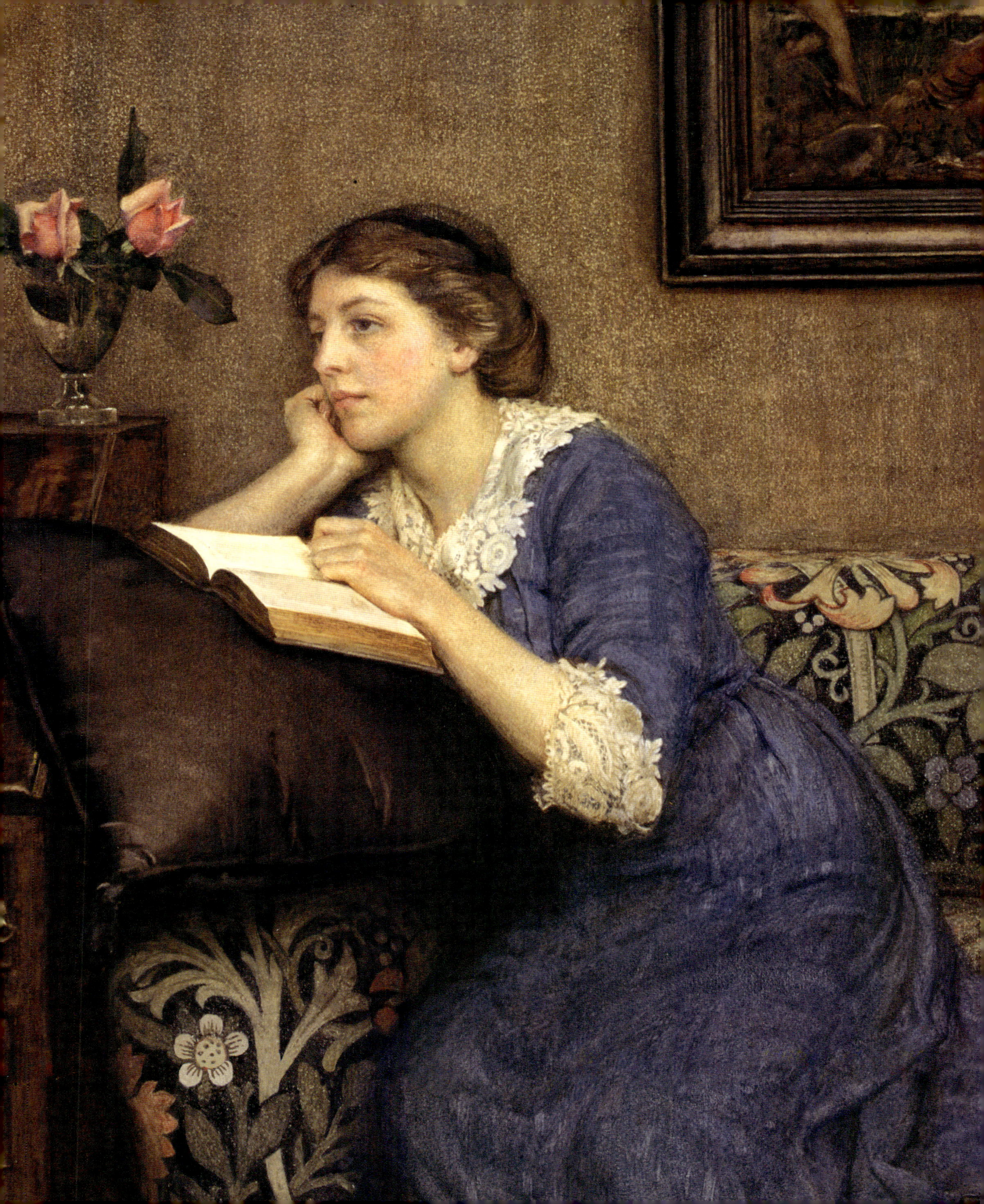

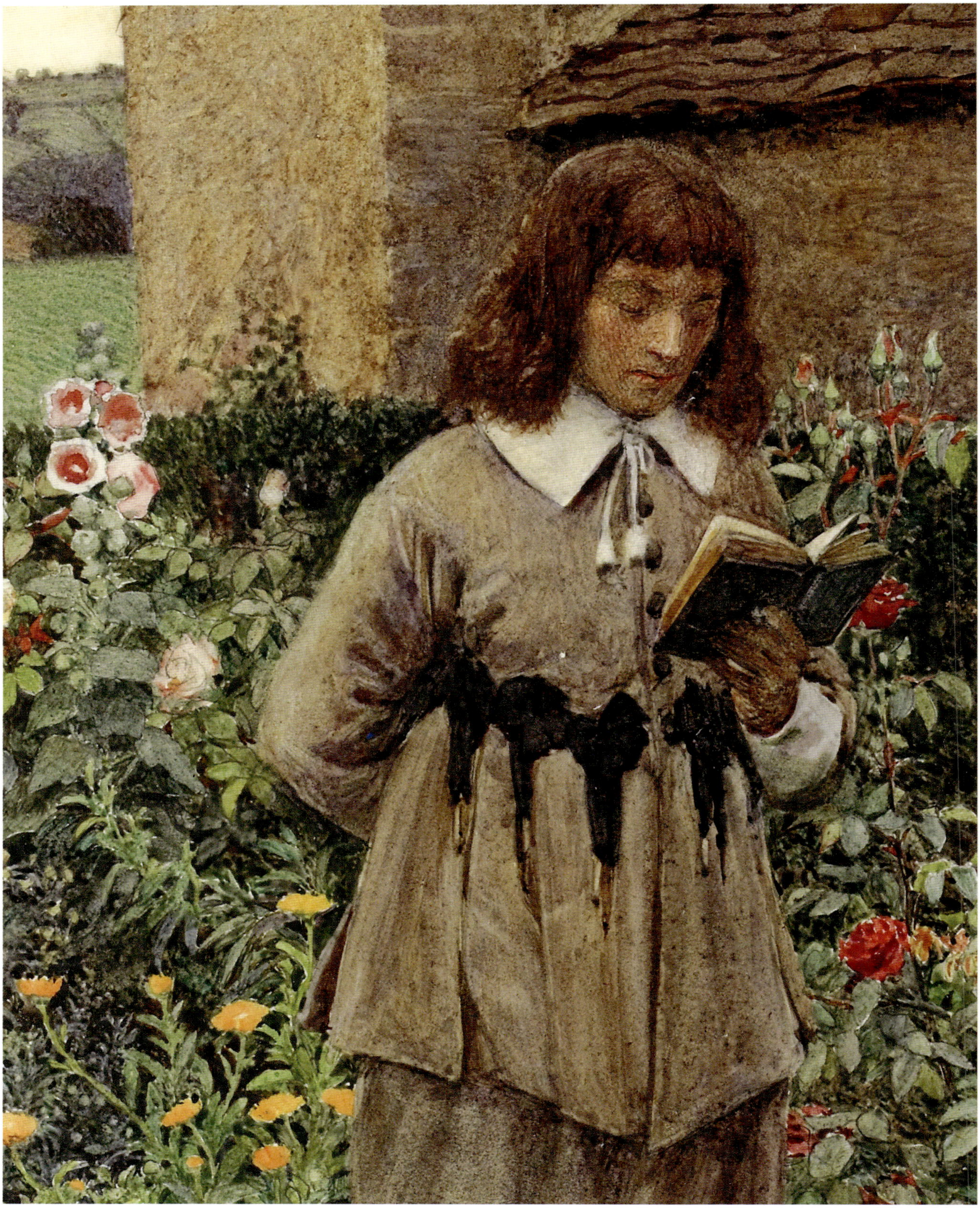

The Wish (Pride and ambition here), 1915

Pen, ink, watercolour, body-colour on paper
36.5 x 25 cm

Ashmolean Museum, University of Oxford

This design for a poem by Abraham Cowley (1618–67) formed part of the set of watercolours Fortescue-Brickdale made for *The Book of Old English Songs and Ballads*, published in 1915. The 'wish' of the title is for "a small house and large garden" to which the narrator could retreat from the "busy world" of the city – this in 1656! True to this theme, the scene is set in the medieval village of Newland in the Wye Valley, a rural nook which the artist knew from her childhood. For many years, her aunt lived in the main street only a few minutes away from the scene depicted here. A truly Pre-Raphaelite appreciation of the vivid detail of nature pushes home the point of the poem.

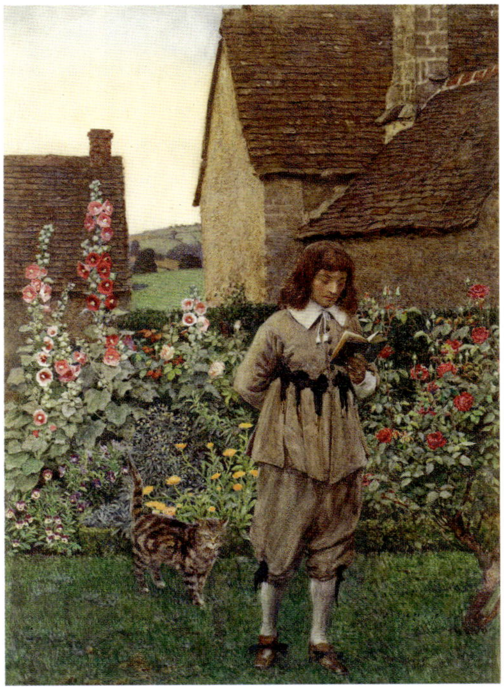

The Book of Old English Songs and Ballads, illustrated by Eleanor Fortescue-Brickdale, Hodder and Stoughton, 1915

Twenty-four colour plates illustrate a range of pre-Victorian texts in Fortescue-Brickdale's seventh coloured book, which contains some of her most successful designs. The Pre-Raphaelite style dominates, with figures set in natural contexts that are observed minutely and rendered in the vivid greens, browns and yellows of the English countryside. Others feature the colourful mosaic of the English garden that Gertrude Jekyll (1843–1932) had reinvented at the turn of the century. The figure of Silvia, from Shakespeare's famous verse, *'Who is Silvia?'*, updates the women of earlier Pre-Raphaelite artists JE Millais, JM Cameron and DG Rossetti, having a certain modernity about her.

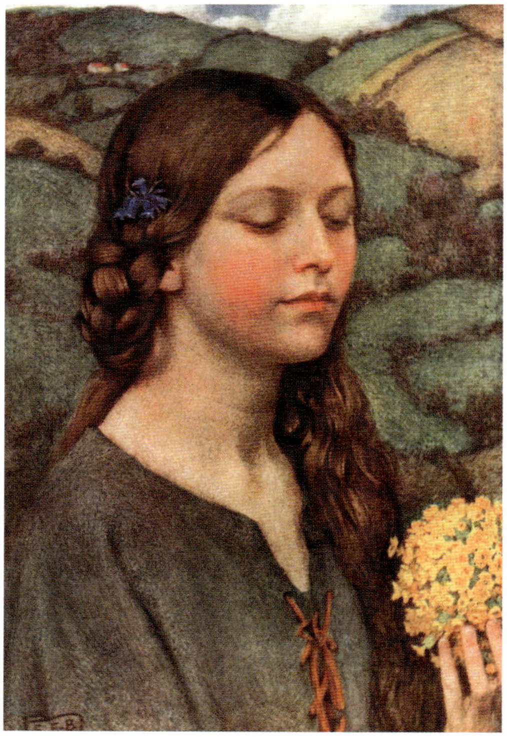

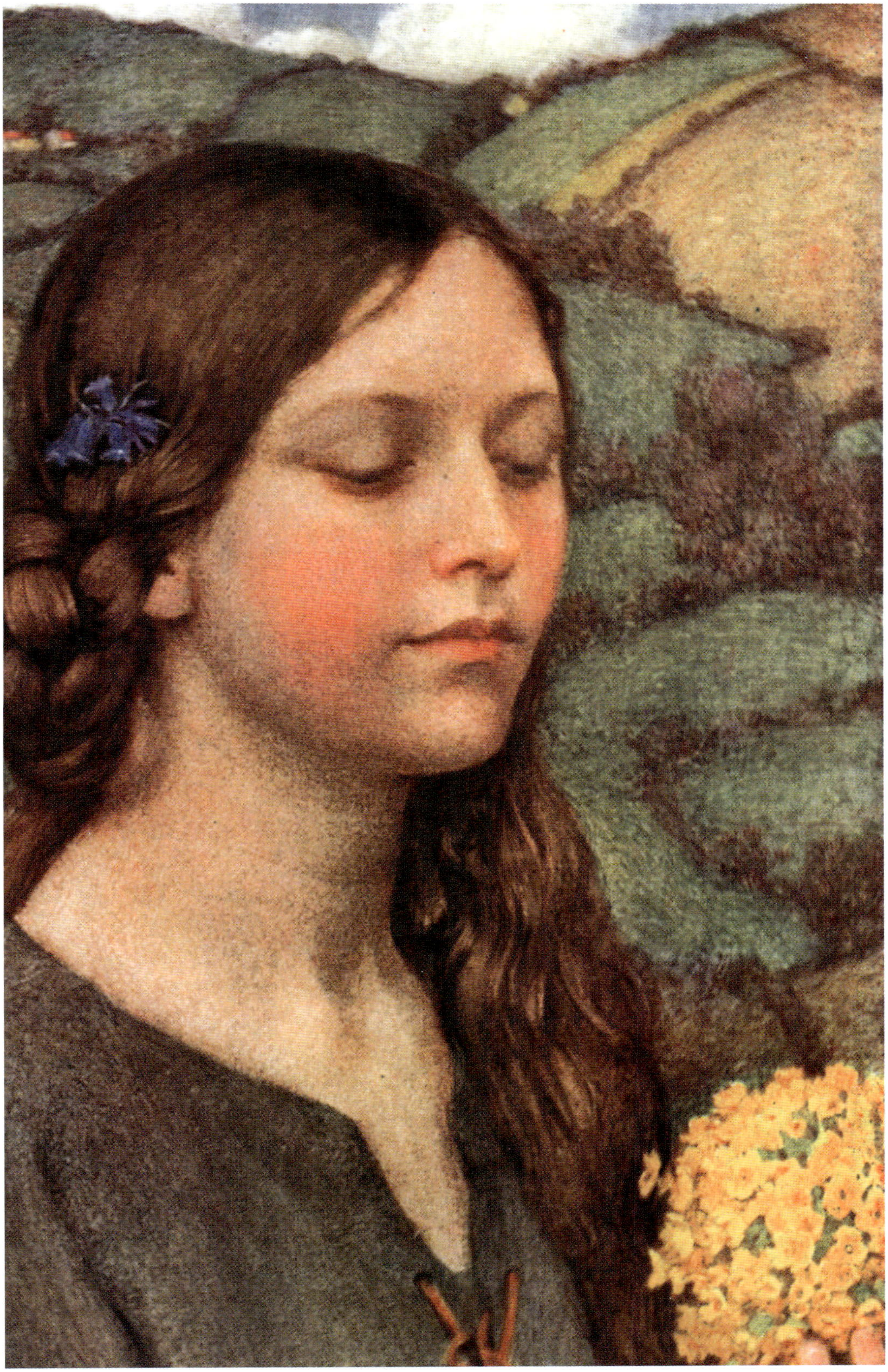

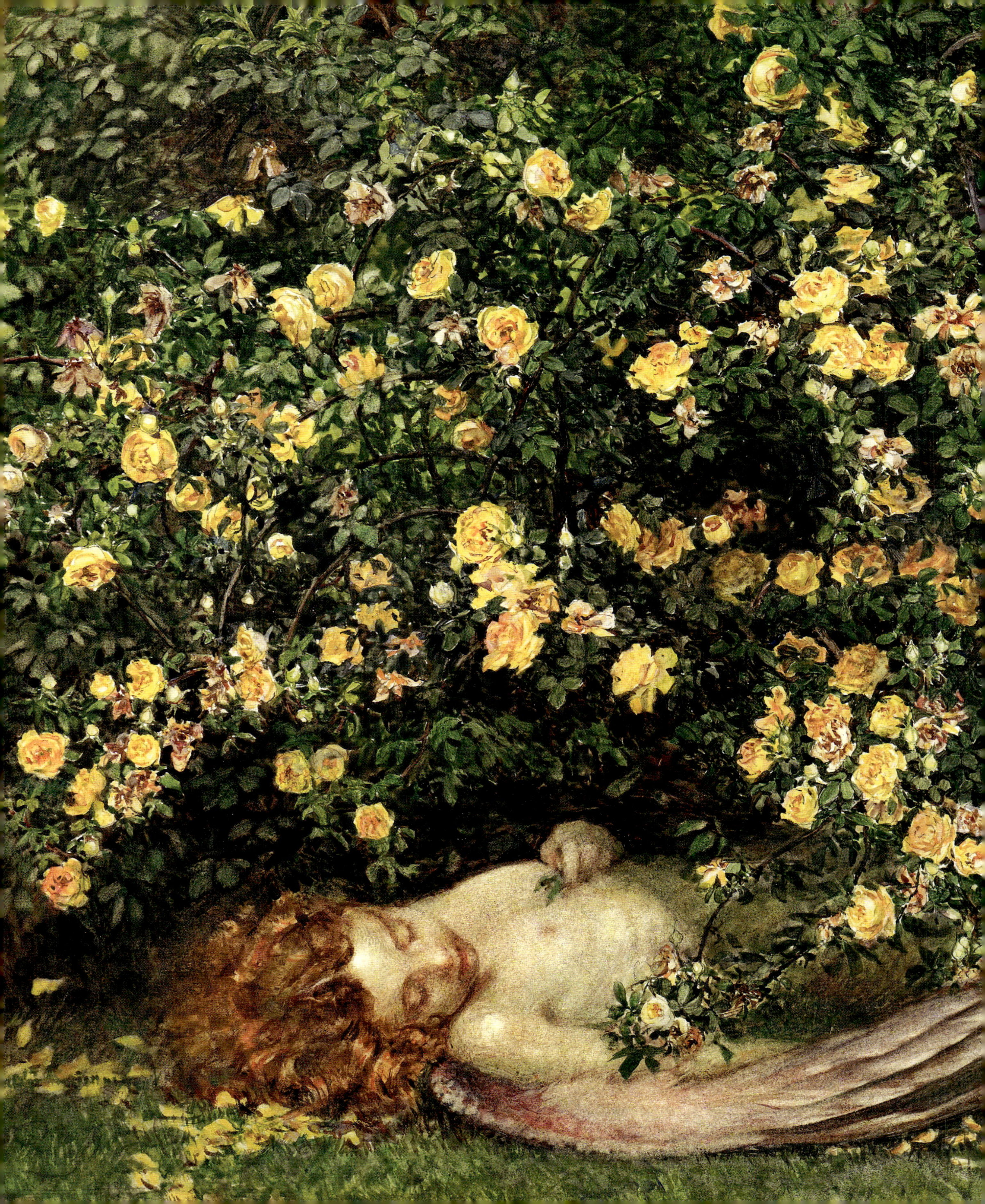

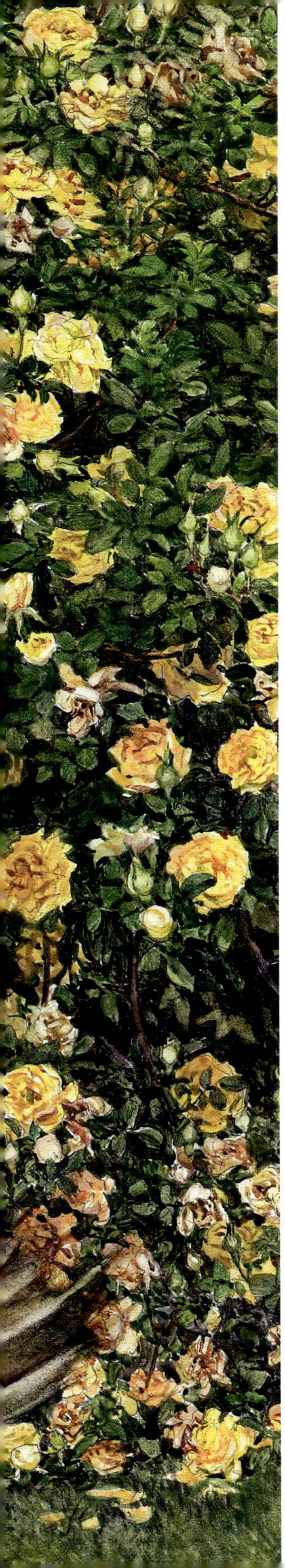

June is Dead, 1915

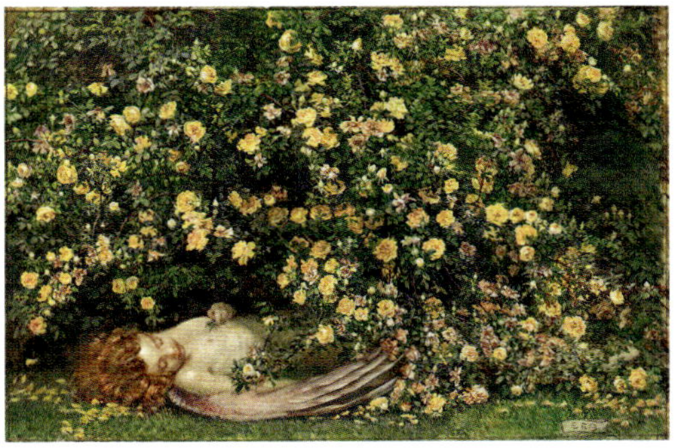

Watercolour on paper, 27.3 x 41 cm

When an artist was elected to a professional society, they were obliged to present a work typical of their output. This is the one Fortescue-Brickdale proffered on her election to the Royal Watercolour Society in 1919 (a process which may have been delayed by the First World War). It includes her characteristically detailed depiction of natural elements, and one of her favourite motifs, the winged cherub, here embodying the month of June. The reference is probably to Robert Browning's poem *'Another Way of Love'*, which appeared in the second volume of his collection *Men and Women*, illustrated by Fortescue-Brickdale in 1908.

Sketch for *Guardian Angel*, 1918

Watercolour over graphite, 22.7 x 13.3 cm

Ashmolean Museum, University of Oxford

This composition was commissioned by the mother of the pioneer aviator and motorist Charles Rolls (1877–1910), who met his death in a flying accident. At this stage of the design, the main pictorial space includes the tiny figure of Icarus accompanied by his father, Daedalus, on an exposed hilltop. He evokes the history of humankind's ambition to fly that links the world of Greek gods and the age of Modernism. The type of the angel is, also, not as eventually painted: this one's bobbed hair and broad forms have a very different character from the head of tight curls and purple shift given to the eventual figure. The viewer is reminded of the artist's eternal problem of whether angels should be rendered male, female or even human at all.

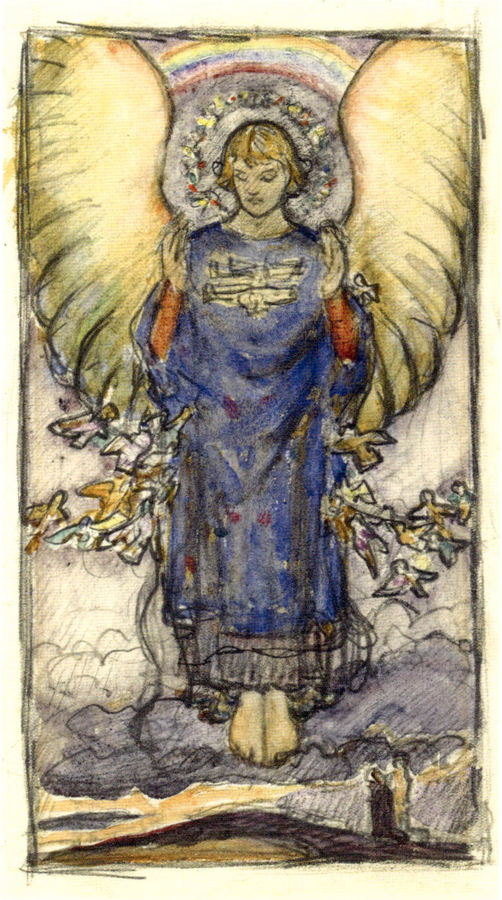

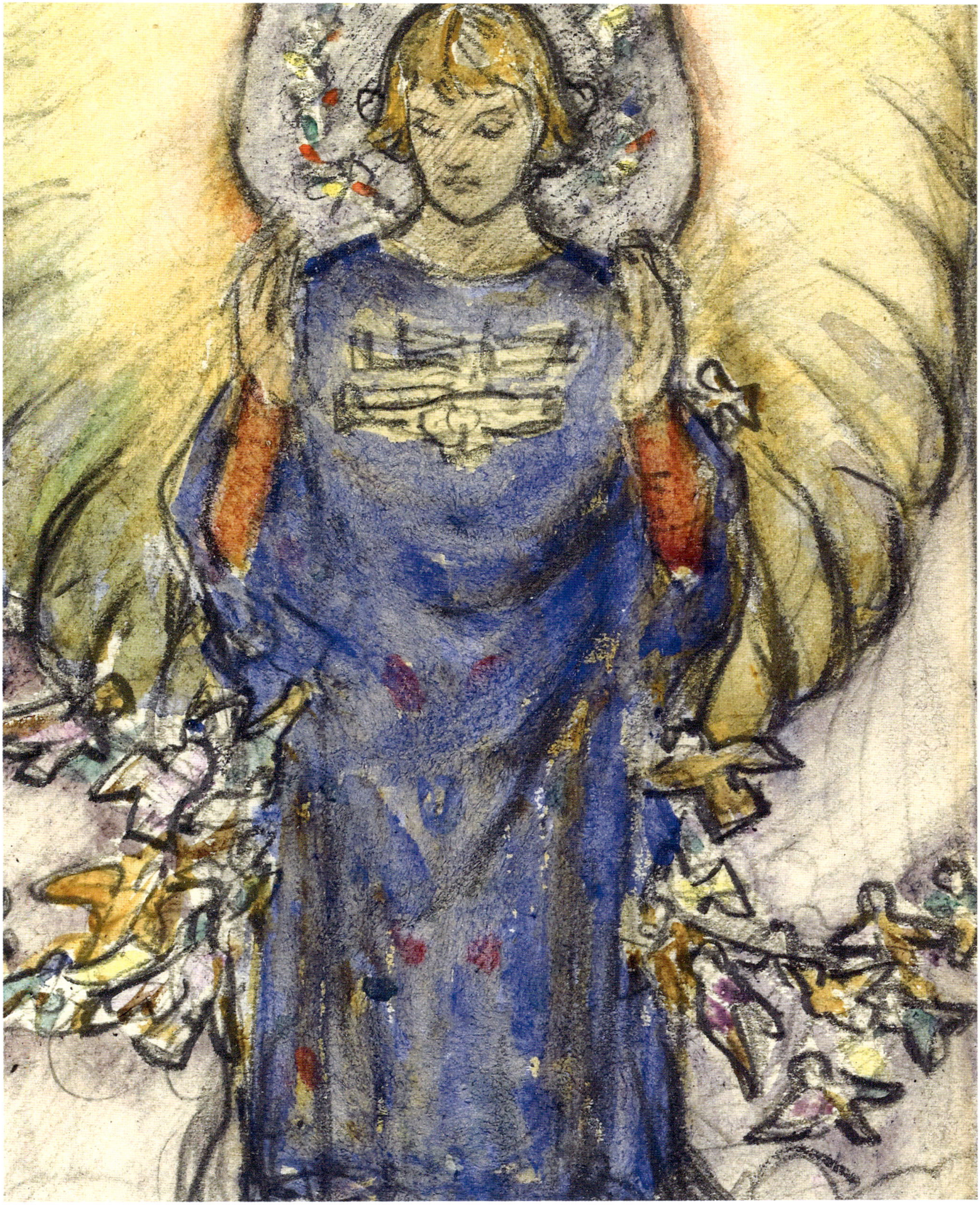

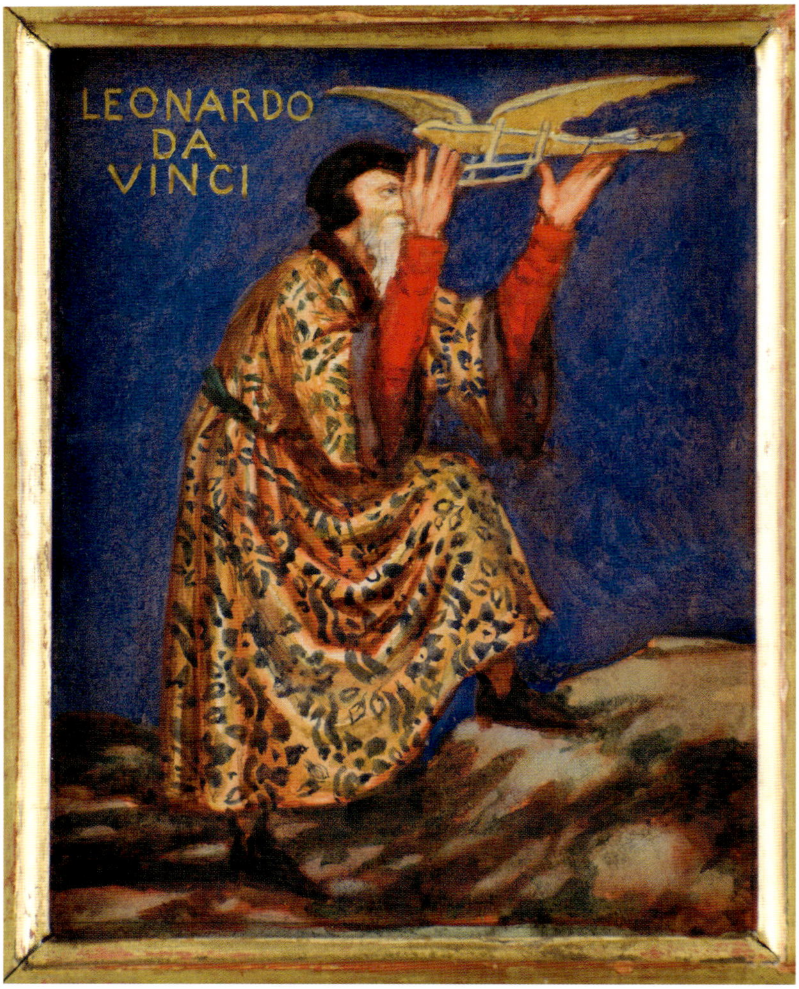
LEONARDO
DA
VINCI

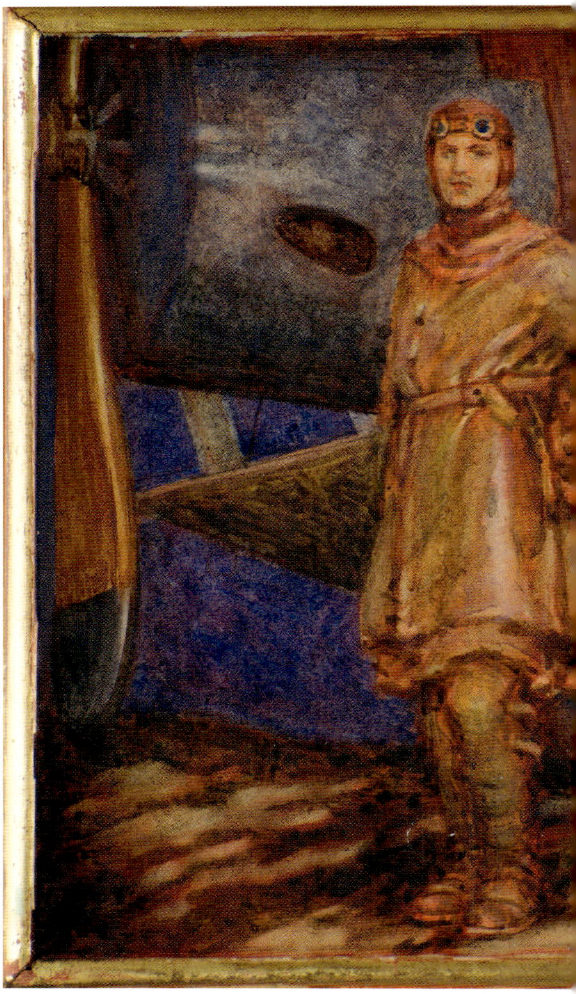

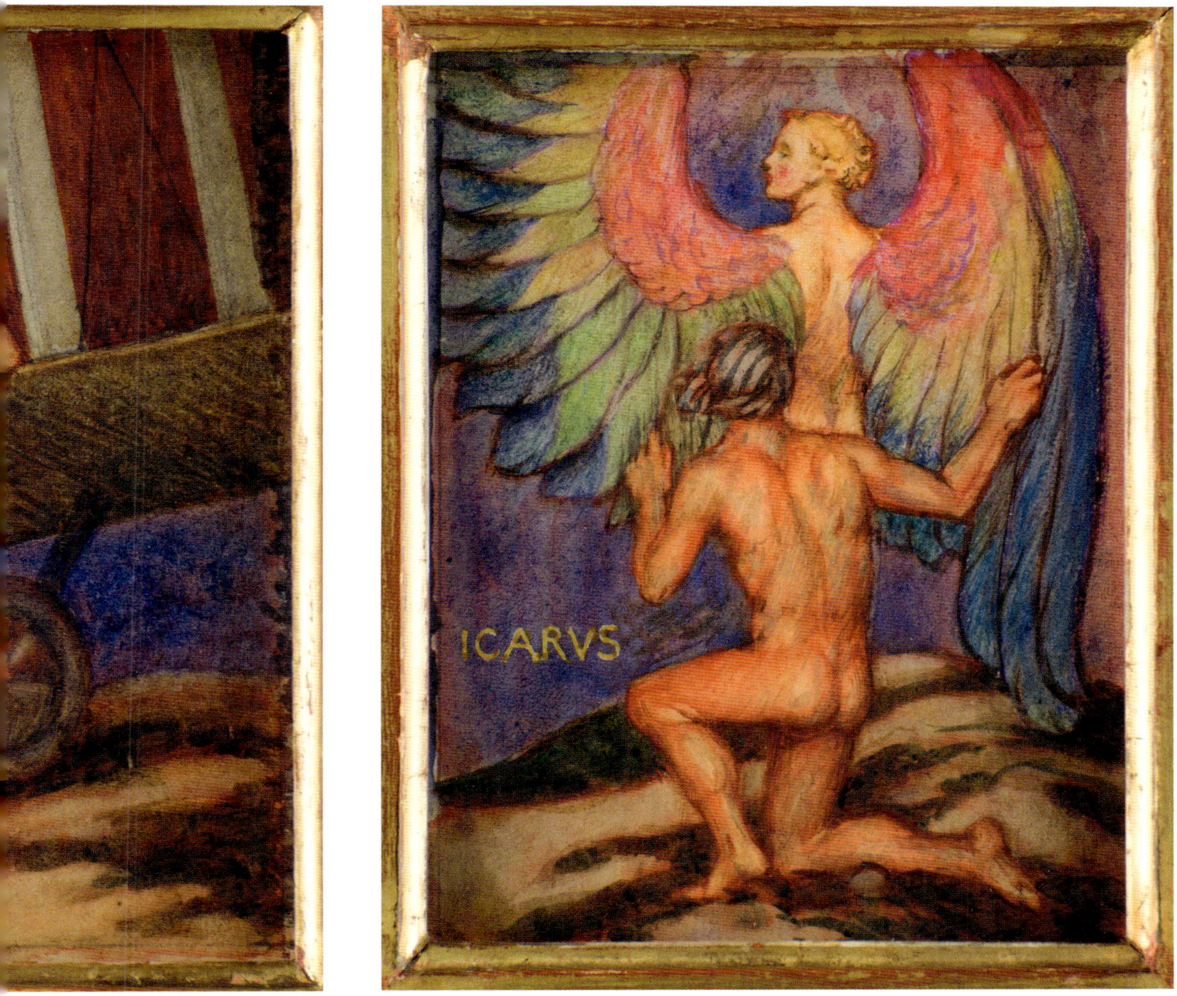

The Guardian Angel (The Genius of Flight), 1918

Watercolour on paper, 77 x 49 cm

The Nelson Museum & Local History Centre, Monmouth

This is a replica (see overleaf) of the original which the artist made on commission from Queen Mary for the London Hospital. The little plane, as if on its final journey from this world to the next, is protected by the hovering angel and accompanied by a flock of birds – nature's prototype which Charles Rolls and other aviators attempted to emulate. At the centre of the predella which has now been added (detailed here), the figure of an early 20th-century airman (not a literal likeness of Rolls) is flanked by two famous predecessors in the development of human flight, Leonardo da Vinci (left) and Icarus (right). The vast emptiness of airspace emphasises the daring of the pioneer aviator's undertaking as he sets off into the uncharted realm of the skies.

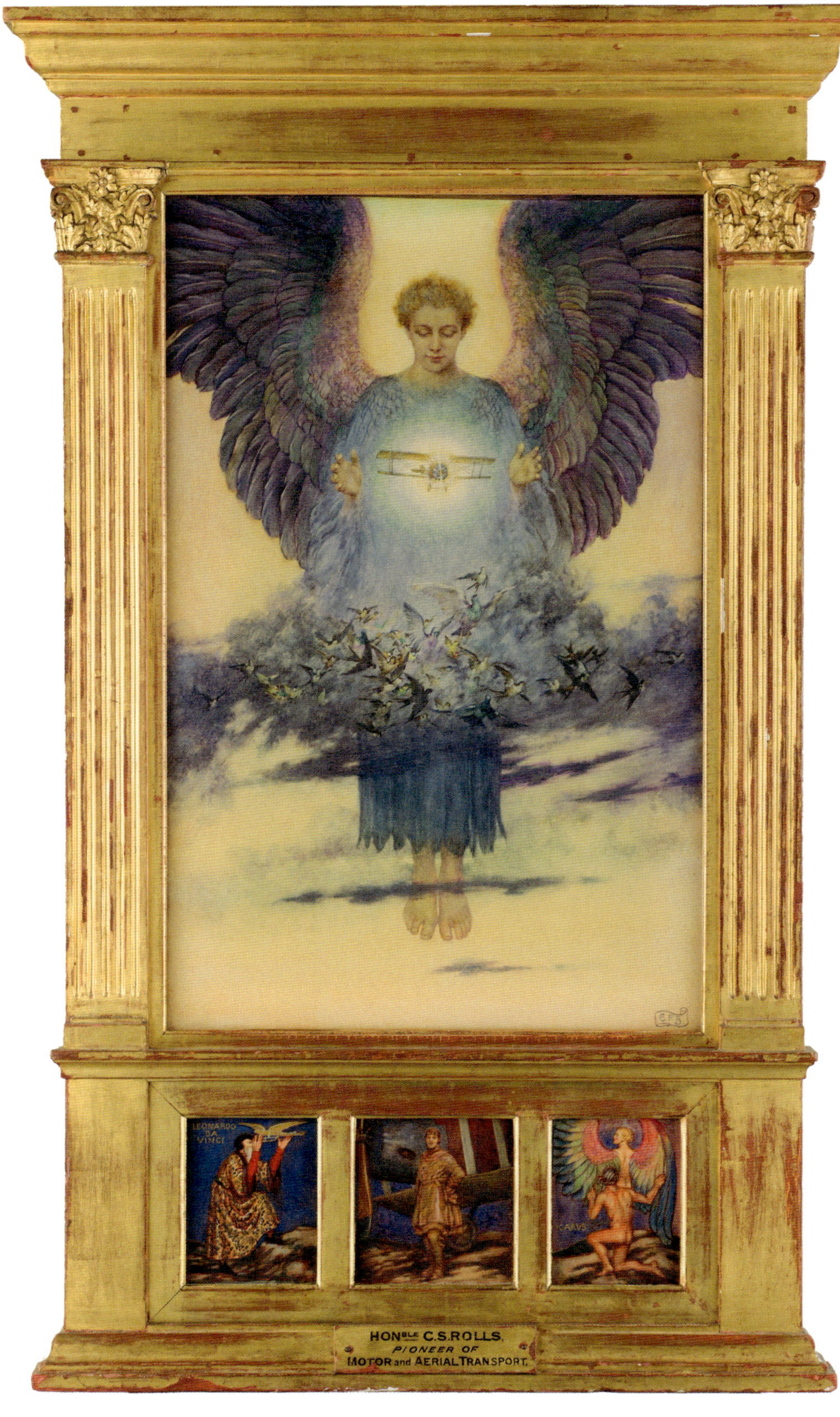
LEONARDO DA VINCI
HON^BLE C.S.ROLLS.
PIONEER OF
MOTOR and AERIAL TRANSPORT.

Eleanor Fortescue Brickdale's Golden Book of Famous Women, Hodder and Stoughton, 1919

Her name above the title and the autograph cover design signalled the widespread public recognition that Fortescue-Brickdale had achieved by this time. Verses by well-known authors from the 16th to the 19th centuries were accompanied by 16 colour plates illustrating heroines as diverse as St Catherine of Siena and Tennyson's Maud. As usual with these projects, an exhibition accompanied the publication: Fortescue-Brickdale's dealers, Ernest Brown and Phillips, put on a show of the watercolour originals at their Leicester Galleries in April 1920.

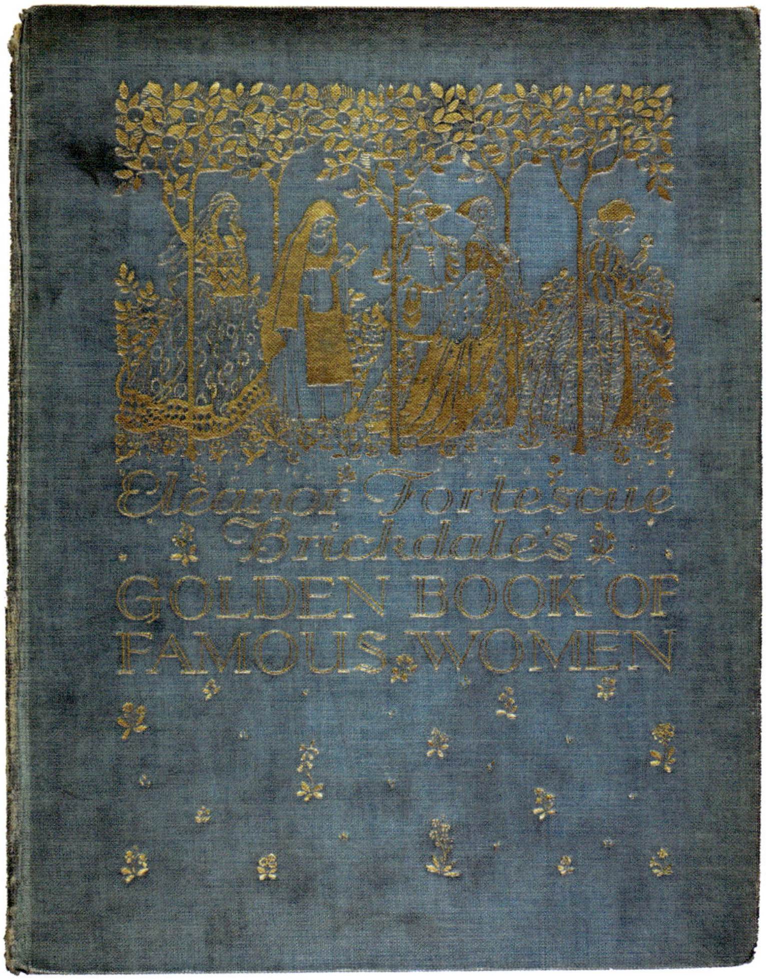

Sketch for *The Forerunner*, 1919–20

Watercolour, pencil on paper, 17.7 x 22.7 cm

This composition celebrates the great artist Leonardo da Vinci (1452–1519), showing him at the court of his patron, Lodovico Sforza, Duke of Milan. It takes its title from a now little known novel by Dmitri Merezhovsky, and Fortescue-Brickdale has taken up the author's key figure of the young boy through whose eyes the narrative unfolds. The composition, like the book, underlines the artist's importance as a role-model and inspiration to future generations. The sketch has been 'squared up' for transfer to the larger canvas. Amongst the handwritten notes beneath the image can be discerned, 'Leonardo born 1452 died 1519' and 'went to Milan first in 1482'.

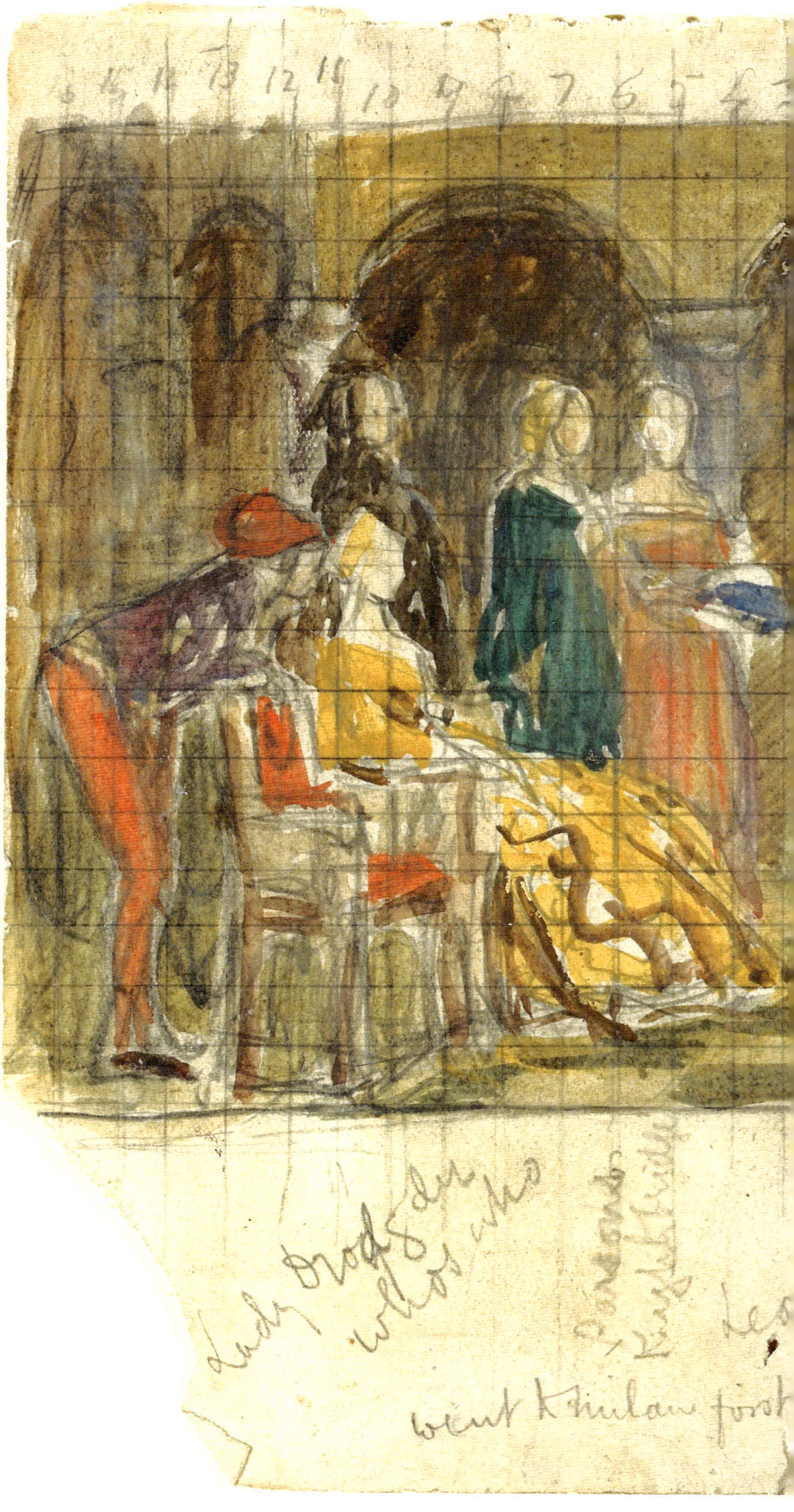

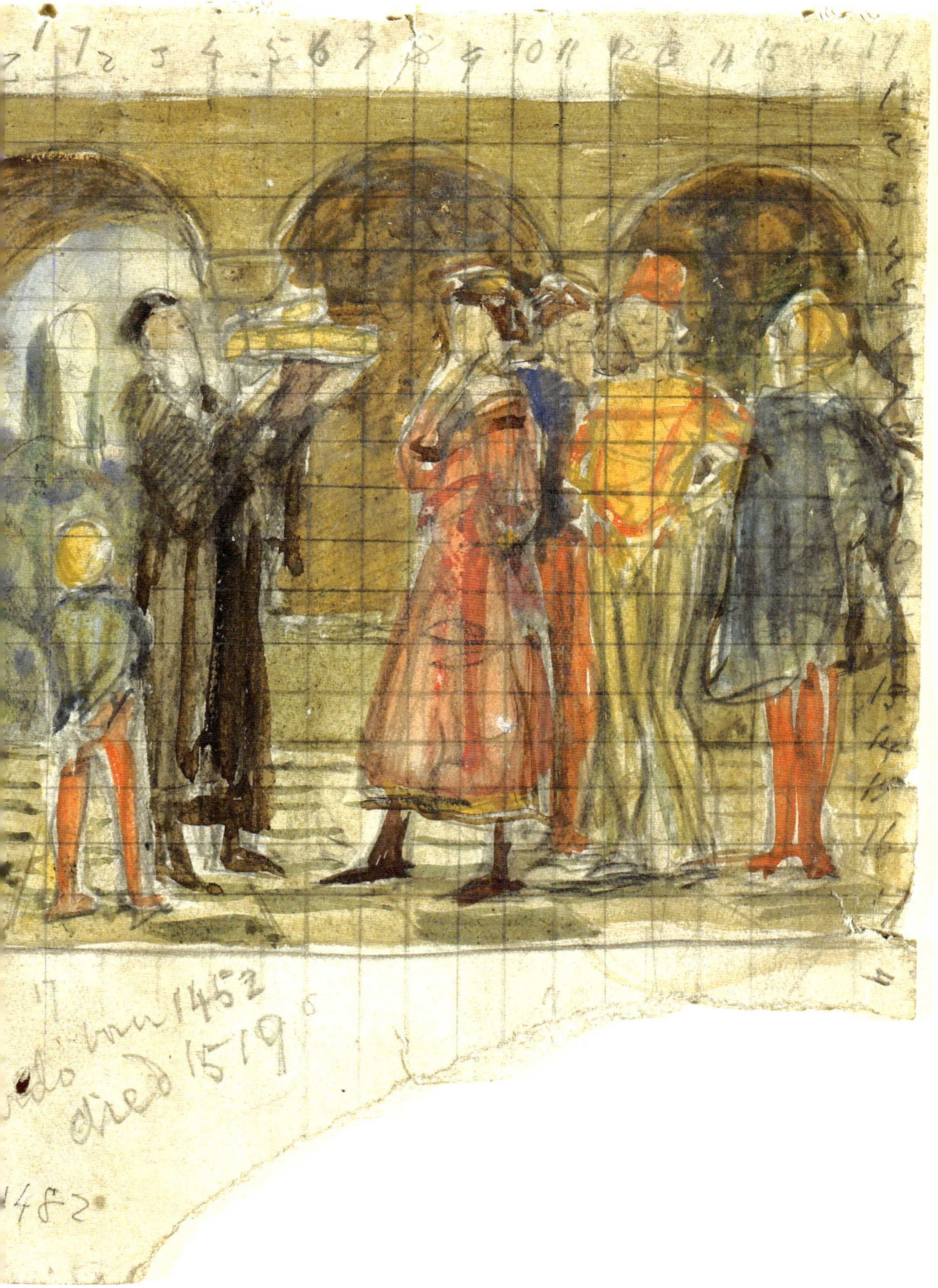
born 1452
died 1519
1482

The Forerunner, 1920

Oil on canvas, 59.6 x 122 cm

Merezhovsky proposes Leonardo as a progressive character whose rationalism and humanism is opposed by sectarian conservatism. In this scene – which Fortescue-Brickdale has invented – Leonardo is shown introducing his latest idea, the flying machine, to Lodovico while other members of his court look on. The famous priest, Savanarola, at far left, stands for the Church's hostility to progress. Lodovico's wife, Beatrice d'Este, and her rival for his affections, Cecilia Galliena, are shown awaiting the outcome of Leonardo's latest challenge to the Duke's tolerance. Brickdale's rendition of these two ladies echoes the famous portraits that Leonardo and his assistant, Ambrogio de Predis, made of them in their lifetimes, further imbuing the work with its hero's spirit.

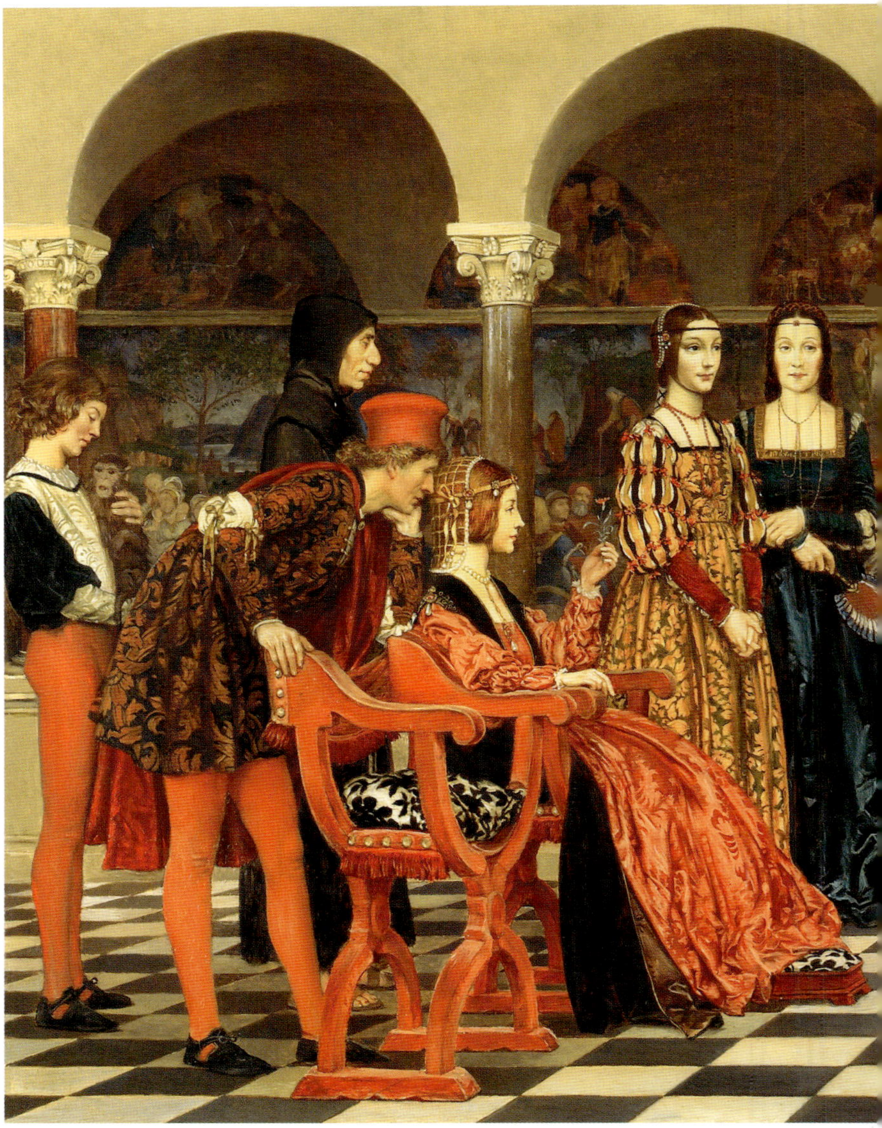

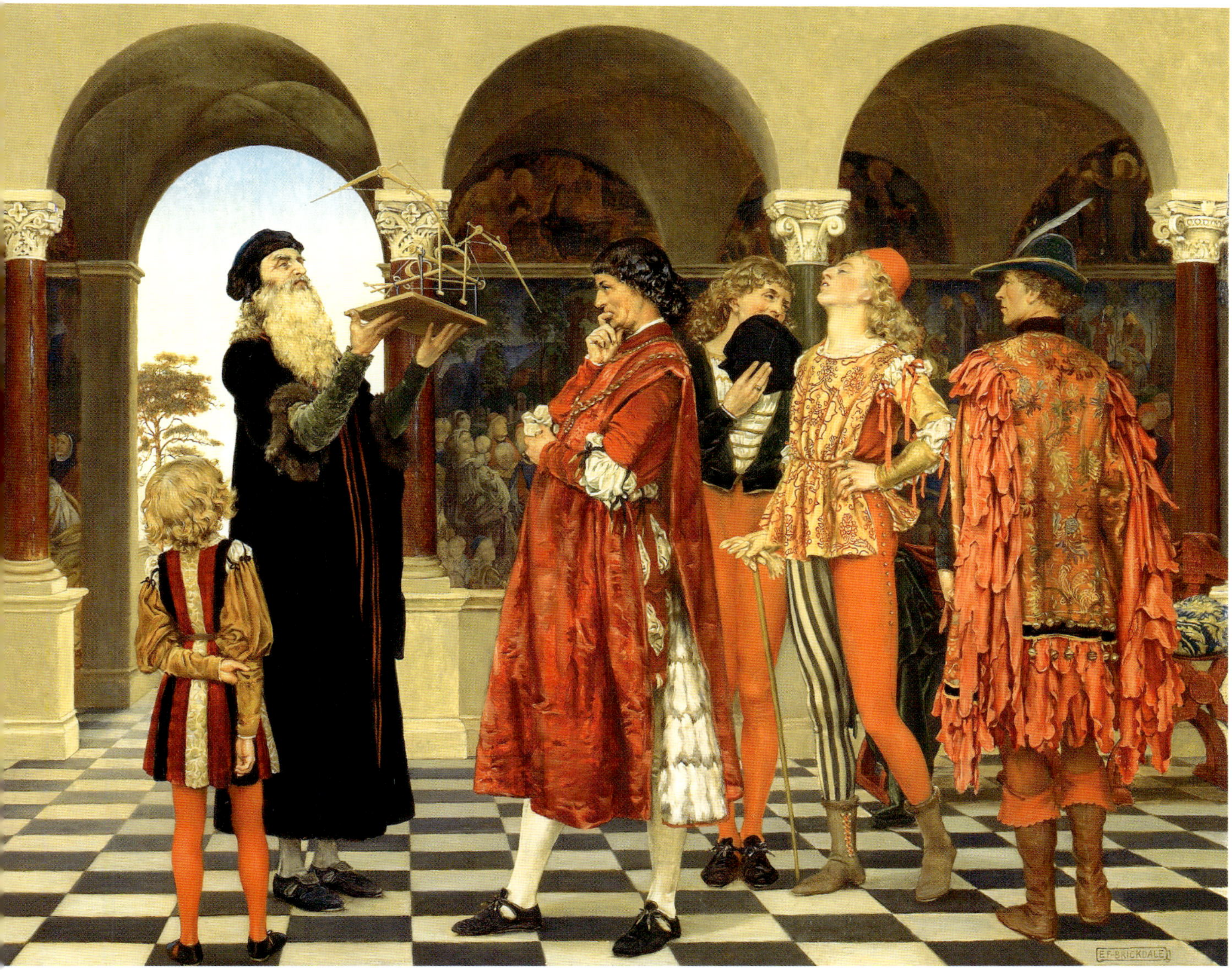
E.F. BRICKDALE

Almshouses at Abingdon, 1920

Watercolour, 30 x 25 cm

Following the Pre-Raphaelite practice of truth to nature, Fortescue-Brickdale used actual locations as settings for her subjects. Here, she has found a suitable background in the town of Abingdon, Berkshire, for her illustration to Robert Herrick's 'The Poetry of Dress' in *Palgrave's Golden Treasury*, published in 1922. The artist often gave away minor works as gifts, and the date inscribed on this study may indicate not when it was made but when it was given to the collector George Clough, whose habit was to write to artists asking for samples of their work.

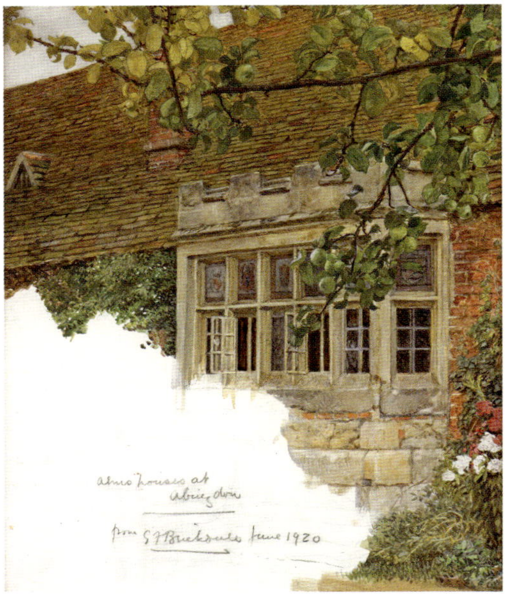

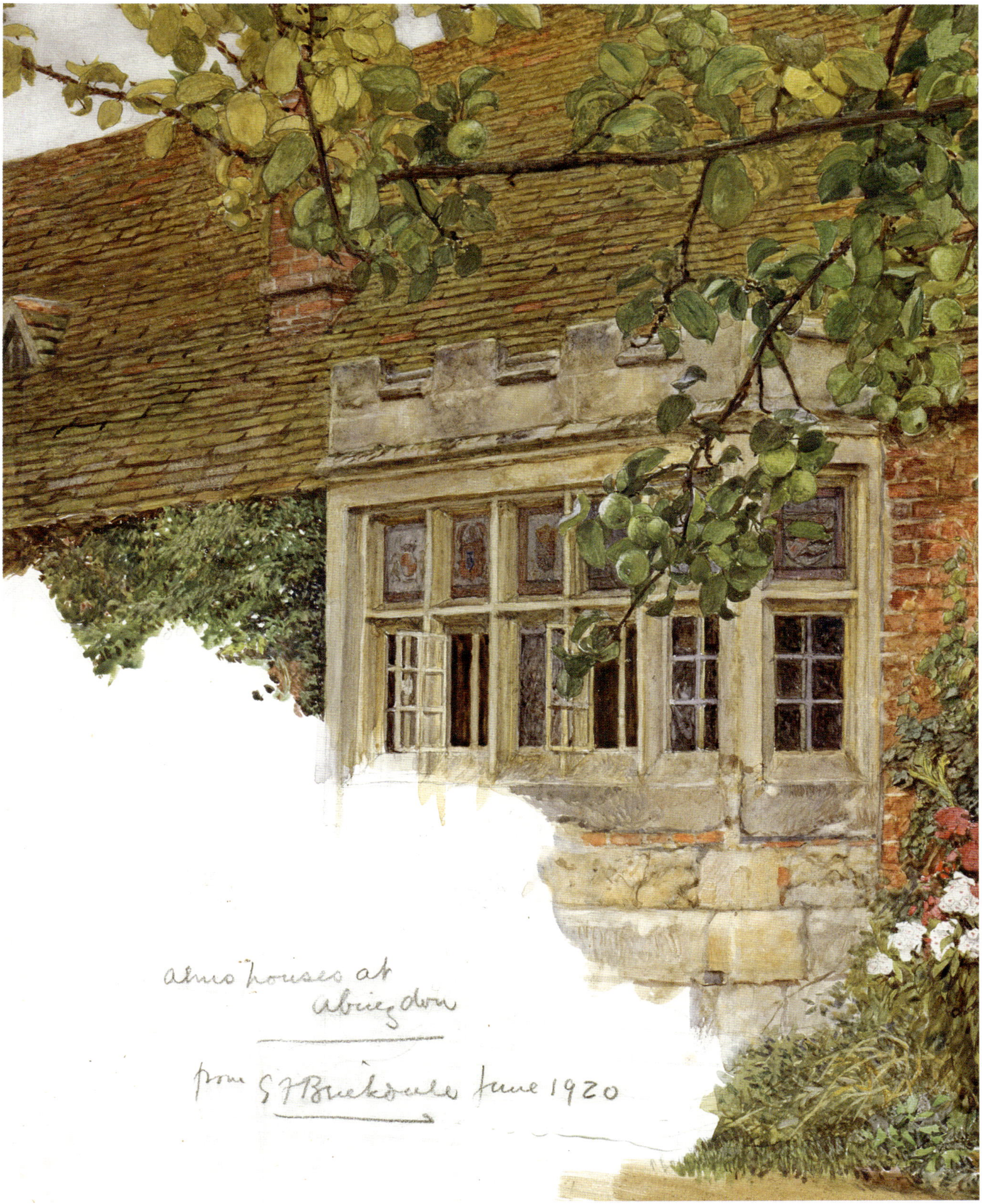
alms houses at
abingdon

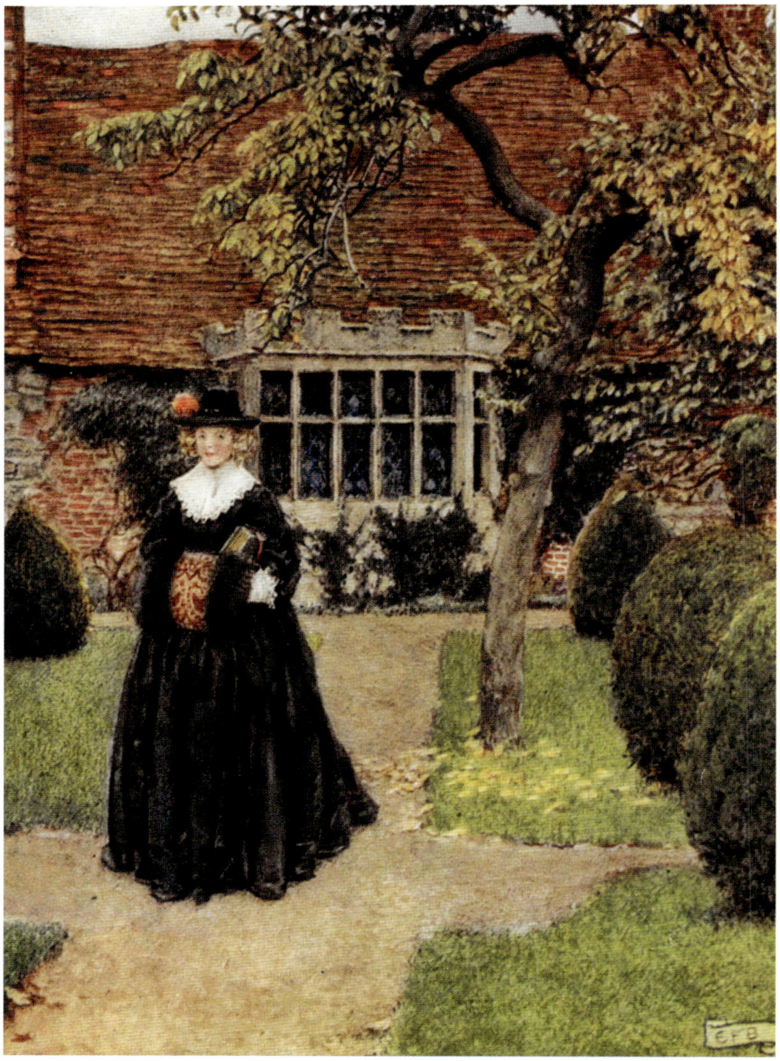

Palgrave's Golden Treasury of Songs and Lyrics, illustrated by Eleanor Fortescue-Brickdale, Hodder and Stoughton, 1924

A mere twelve colour plates in a 460-page book perhaps reflects the ill health that Fortescue-Brickdale suffered in the early 1920s. The best of the plates revive the approach of the *Songs and Ballads* selection, as here, with a single figure set in a scene of minutely observed nature or domestic architecture. Fortescue-Brickdale's wide-ranging knowledge of historical costume – a key component in her work throughout her career – is particularly apt for 'When in silks my Julia goes', as the poem's theme is the seductiveness of the heroine's clothing.

Portrait of Charles Fortescue-Brickdale, 1924

Oil on canvas, 49 x 37 cm

Photograph reproduced with kind permission of HM Land Registry Museum, Peterborough

Charles Fortescue-Brickdale (1857–1944) was Eleanor's elder brother. They shared an interest in art, and Charles was a keen amateur artist. In his professional life he was a barrister, specialising in land law. He spent all but the first five years of his career at His Majesty's Land Registry, which he almost single-handedly modernised. For this service he was knighted in 1911. This portrait was made to mark his retirement in 1923, and in it he wears the court dress which, as Chief Registrar, he would have worn on ceremonial occasions. Another version of this portrait appears in his sister's valedictory composition *Mary for all Generations* (1929–30).

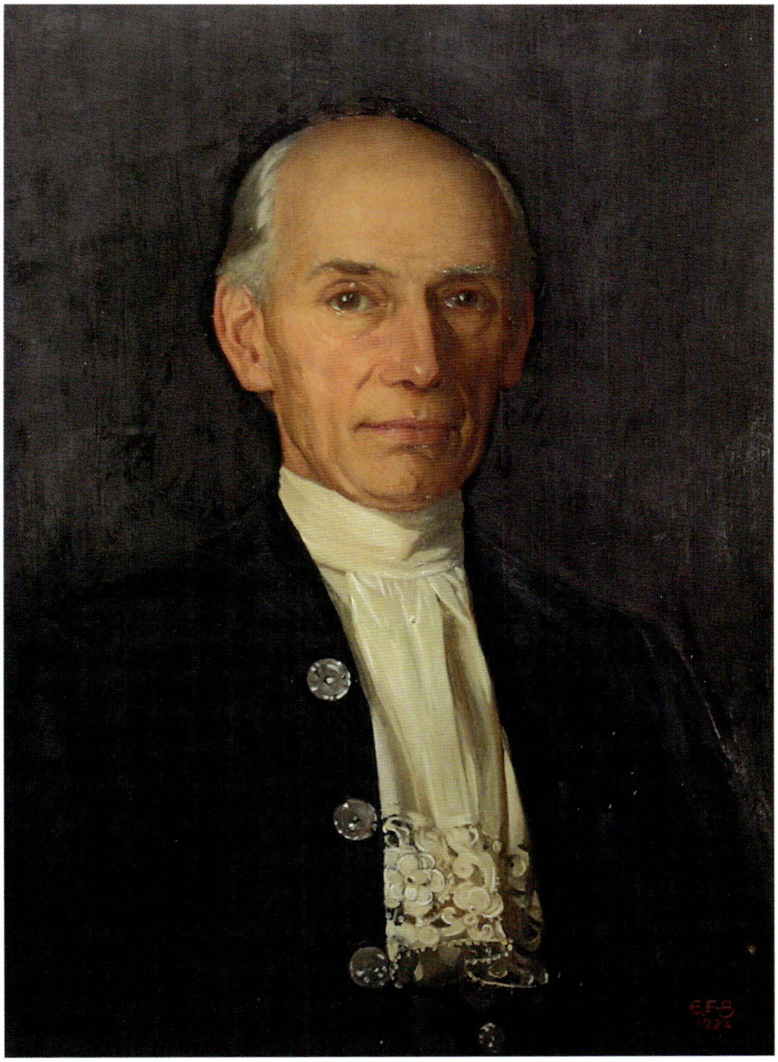

The Prior's Niece, about 1932

Watercolour on paper, 37.4 x 26.5 cm

Image courtesy The Royal Pavilion and Museums, Brighton & Hove

This work takes its subject from the poems of Robert Browning. The prior's niece is a minor character in the poem *Fra Lippo Lippi*, in the *Men and Women* collection that Fortescue-Brickdale illustrated in 1909 (though this design was not in that selection). The artist shows the monk artist - whom Browning proposes as torn between worldly pleasures and religious duties - sketching the attractive young woman as she visits her uncle in the cloister. His subsequent rendition of her is praised by his brother monks (seen in the background) for its likeness, though disapproved as an unworthy subject for a devout artist.

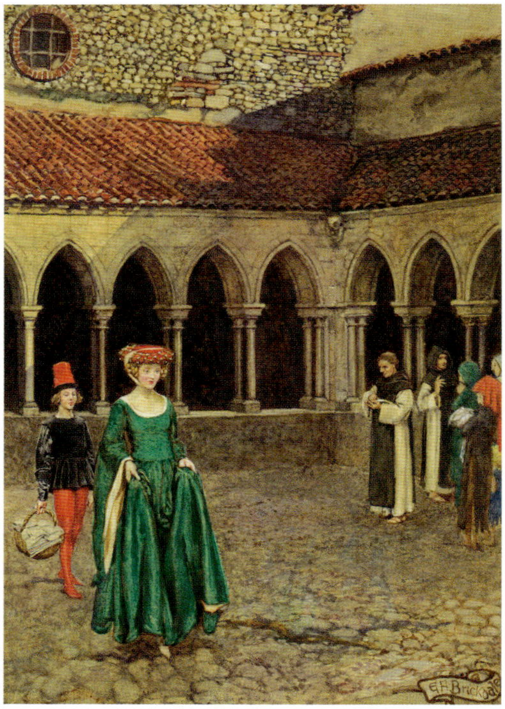

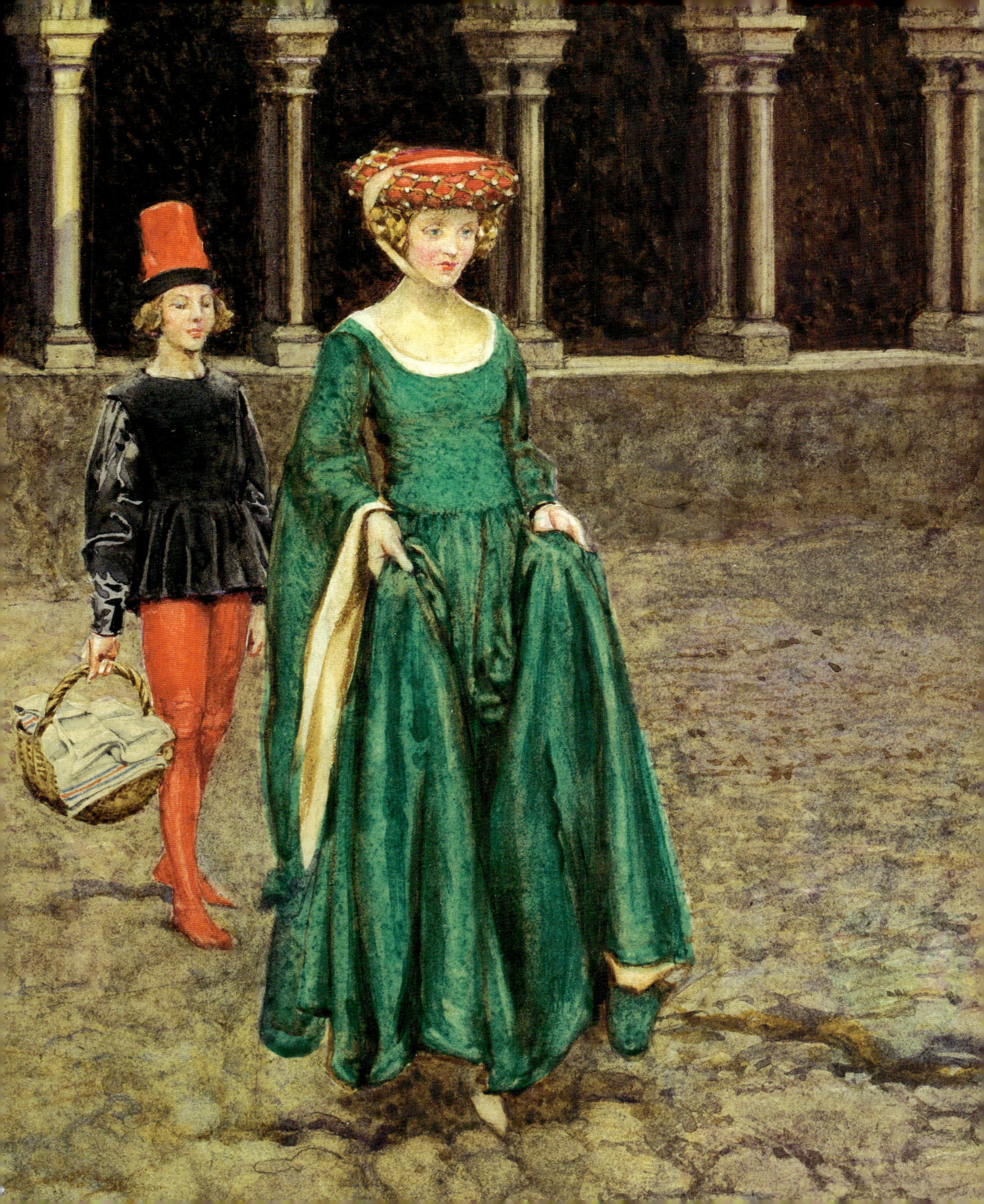

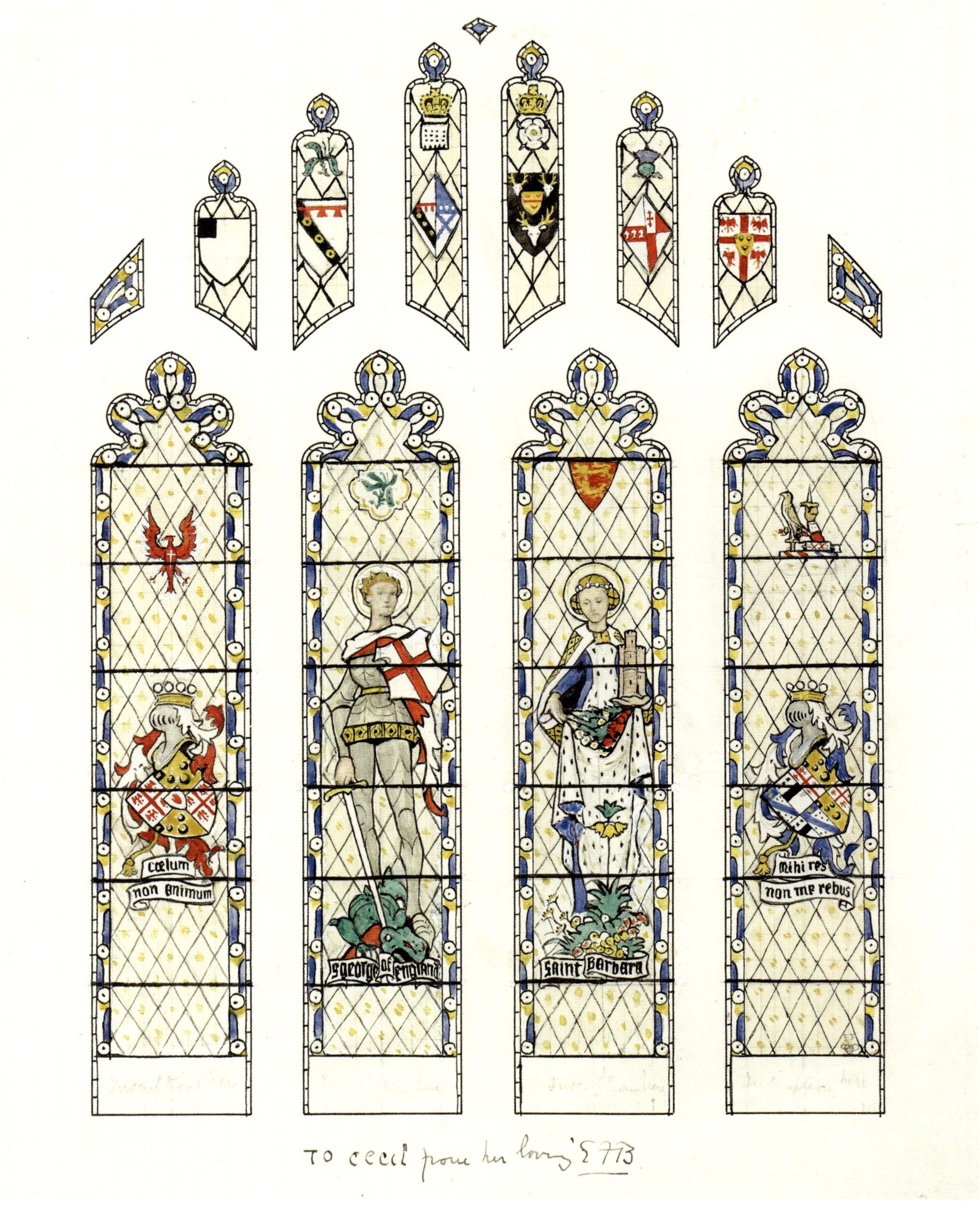
cœlum
non animum
S. George of England
Saint Barbara
mihi res
non me rebus

Design for a Window in Chew Magna church, 1934

Ink, watercolour on paper, 34.8 x 27 cm

Ashmolean Museum, University of Oxford

Fortescue-Brickdale had been working in stained glass for some 20 years when she executed this design for the Strachey chapel in St Andrew's church, Chew Magna, Somerset. The two saints, George and Barbara, commemorate Edward Strachey, MP for South Somerset, and his wife Frances, whose death in 1931 prompted the commission. There are some intriguing differences between this design - one of two in existence, both held by the Ashmolean Museum - and the window as executed. Chiefly, the female saint's identification was changed to Elisabeth of Hungary (while retaining Barbara's attributes), and St George's legend became 'in deo et rege' ('for god and king') instead of his name.

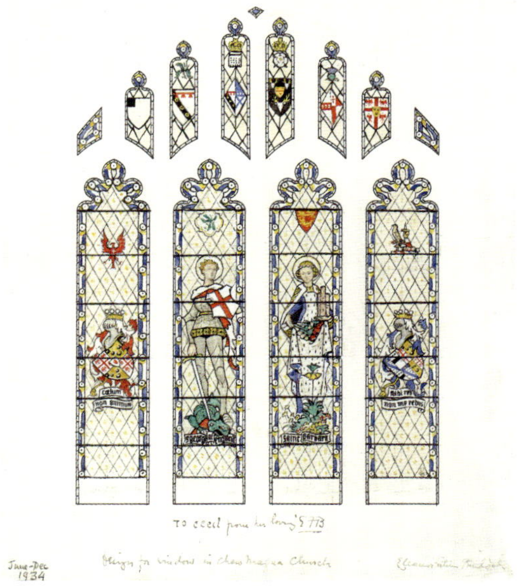

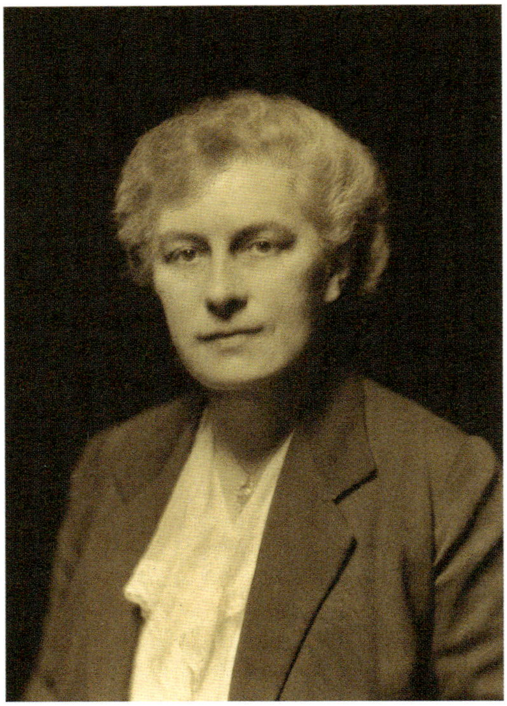

Eleanor Fortescue-Brickdale,
about 1920-1930,
© Private collection